Recipes from the Vineyards of Oregon

Leslie J. Whipple

— A Maverick Publication —

ISBN 0-89288-247-6
Library of Congress Catalog Card Number: 94-79779

Credits

Cover Photo Design and Food Styling—Leslie J. Whipple

Layout and Design—Bridget R. Wise

Maps courtesy of the Oregon Wine Advisory Board

Leaded glass windows (on cover) courtesy of Bob Harrison

Antique Prints—Nineteenth Century Imprints (503) 234-3538

Maverick Publications
P.O. Box 5007
Bend, Oregon 97708

To Mom and Dad, with all my love.

Acknowledgments

I would like to express my gratitude and appreciation to
Jerry Crowley who made everything possible.

I also wish to thank: Stewart M. Whipple

Marcia J. Whipple

Doran Whipple

Helen Hall

Richard Mansfield

Mark McChrystal

Micheal Straus

Gary Asher

Tom Healy

Bridget Wise

H. Bruce Miller

Larry Challacomb

Elisabeth Burdon

This book would not have been possible without the contributions and cooperation of the many people who own and work with the wineries of Oregon, who made their recipes, stories and expertise available to *Recipes from the Vineyards of Oregon*. I wish to thank them all for their generosity.

Table of Contents

NORTH WILLAMETTE REGION

South Willamette Region

Umpqua Region

Rogue Region

Appendices

From wine what sudden
friendship springs!

JOHN GAY

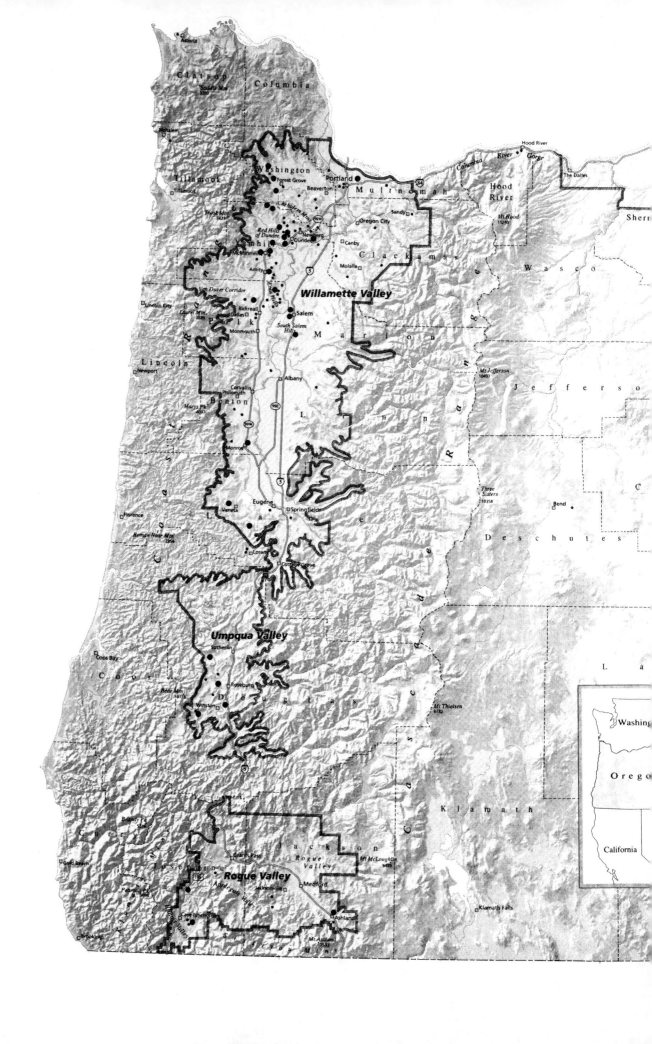

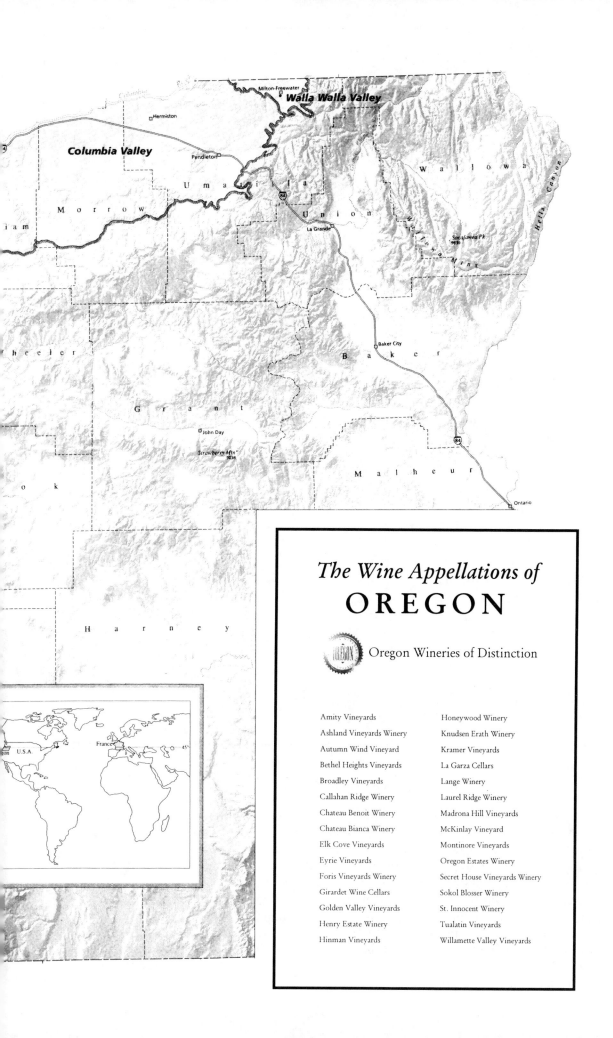

Milton-Freewater

Walla Walla Valley

Hermiston

Columbia Valley

Pendleton

U m a t i l l a

M o r r o w

iam

W a l l o w a

Hells Canyon

U n i o n

La Grande

Wallowa Mtns

Sacajawea Pk
9830

W h e e l e r

B a k e r

Baker City

G r a n t

John Day

Strawberry Mtn
9038

o k

M a l h e u r

Ontario

H a r n e y

U.S.A.

France

45°

The Wine Appellations of
OREGON

Oregon Wineries of Distinction

Amity Vineyards

Ashland Vineyards Winery

Autumn Wind Vineyard

Bethel Heights Vineyards

Broadley Vineyards

Callahan Ridge Winery

Chateau Benoit Winery

Chateau Bianca Winery

Elk Cove Vineyards

Eyrie Vineyards

Foris Vineyards Winery

Girardet Wine Cellars

Golden Valley Vineyards

Henry Estate Winery

Hinman Vineyards

Honeywood Winery

Knudsen Erath Winery

Kramer Vineyards

La Garza Cellars

Lange Winery

Laurel Ridge Winery

Madrona Hill Vineyards

McKinlay Vineyard

Montinore Vineyards

Oregon Estates Winery

Secret House Vineyards Winery

Sokol Blosser Winery

St. Innocent Winery

Tualatin Vineyards

Willamette Valley Vineyards

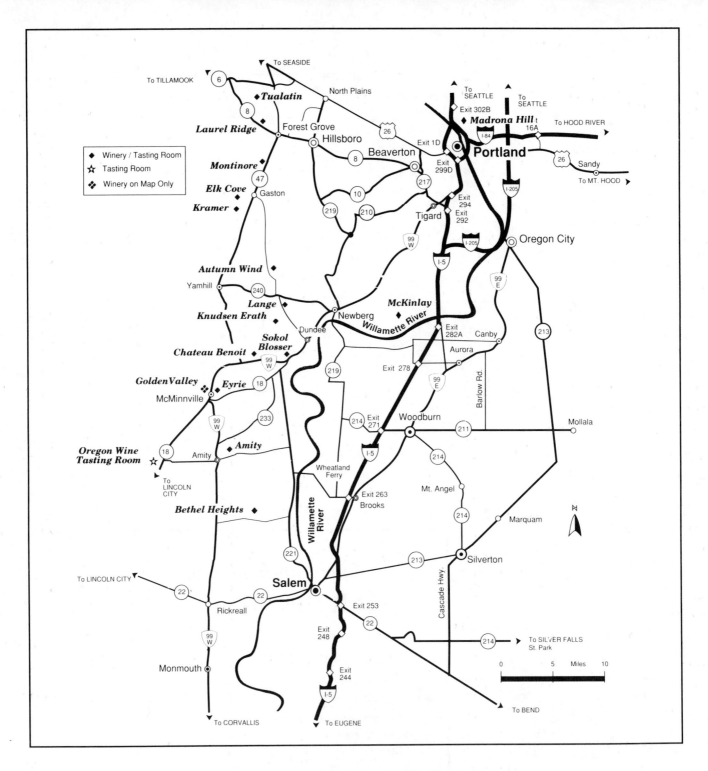

The Willamette Valley

The Willamette Valley, Oregon's coolest wine appellation, is the source for most of the state's winegrapes. Approximately 60 miles wide at its greatest breadth, the Willamette River Valley runs south to north, approximately 100 miles from Eugene to the Columbia River at Portland. The main highway artery of the state, Interstate 5, follows the river. The center of the valley is approximately 50 miles east of the Pacific Ocean which provides marine air influence depending on weather conditions and local formations of the Coastal Range Mountains. Most of the approximately 40 inches of annual rainfall occurs during the mild winter months. Summers are relatively warm and dry. Vineyards are typically located on benchland hillsides at the western margin of the valley. Distinct subregions can be identified including the Red Hills of Dundee southwest of Portland, the Eola Hills northwest of Salem, the South Salem Hills, and the area west of Eugene near the town of Veneta.

North Willamette Region

Menu

A Wine Tasting Dinner

*Amity Vineyards Dry
Gewürztraminer*
**A Royal Garlic
Toast Treat**

———

Amity Vineyards Dry Riesling
Curried Crab Turnovers

———

*Amity Vineyards
Winemakers Reserve Pinot Noir*
**Lamb Chops with Plums
and Chanterelles**

———

*Amity Vineyards
Willamette Valley Pinot Noir*
**Duck Breast Salad
with Pinot Noir Dressing**

———

*Amity Vineyards Juliyard Vineyards
Late Harvest Riesling*
**Drunken Fruit over
Pound Cake**

Amity Vineyards

Amity has gained a reputation, both in the United States and abroad, for wines of structure, complexity and simple excellence. Winemaker Myron Redford moved to Oregon in 1974 with a dream for a winery that would specialize in Burgundian style Pinots. Pinot Noir has since become the flagship wine at Amity. Working with up to 32 separate and distinct lots of wine, Winemaker Redford smells, tastes and blends to create two to four Pinot Noir releases in a vintage. Appealing to a wide range of Pinot drinkers, they range from the "Oregon, Red Label," soft and approachable, to the "Gold Label, Winemaker's Reserve"—made only in exceptional years and designed for long aging in the tradition of Grand Cru Burgundies.

Amity is also known for Dry Gewürztraminers and Rieslings as well as new varietals to the United States such as Gamay Noir. It also introduced Oregon's first sulfite free wine from organic grapes, Eco Wine. It is a Pinot Noir. The Gewürztraminers are made in the Alsatian style. Visitors from that region have stated: "I never thought I would ever taste a Gewürztraminer outside of Alsace that would remind me of Alsace." Rieslings are made both in the dry and late harvest styles. These wines consistently win Gold medals and high ratings. Amity was the first American winery to produce Gamay Noir, the variety found in the wines of Beaujolais. The grapes were grown from cuttings provided to Oregon by the French government. This wine is now in national distribution and becoming an increasingly popular wine, especially served slightly chilled in the summer.

The winery itself is situated atop the Amity hills and commands a spectacular view of the Oregon Coast Range and the Willamette Valley.

Food and wine are constant themes here at Amity Vineyards. Myron and I entertain a great deal and love that special feeling when the wines and foods are matched with new and old friends. Amity, after all, means friendship. This menu is designed to show one way to match wine and foods while tasting a variety of wines. I have always loved having several varieties of wines with a meal. These recipes will be for 4 to 6 people for ease of preparation and also because there are 25 ounces of wine in a standard 750 ml bottle, which means each person will get a good glass of wine from a bottle and have some to spare for the cook. Yes, I use the wine I will serve in cooking. I would never use a wine I would not drink in a dish, unless I was making vinegar. The flavors you taste in the wine will be accentuated in the cooking. Besides, a cook always needs a glass of wine when preparing a dinner party.

The Willamette Valley grows wonderful orchard crops, hazelnuts, garlic, berries, wild and cultivated mushrooms and, of course, is famous for wine grapes. We also have wonderful salmon, trout, lamb and veal. So the possibilities are endless. On our home farm, Myron and I grow organic plums, berries and garlic, as well as most of our herbs. So I have chosen recipes using these ingredients.

A Royal Garlic Toast Treat

This is a wonderful starter for 6 to 8 people or two garlic lovers. A great starter for a lamb dinner. It is not low fat, but has a high taste rating.

6 tablespoons olive oil
6 tablespoons unsalted butter
50 cloves garlic, peeled
1-1/2 cups 1993 Amity Vineyards
    Gewürztraminer
Freshly ground pepper
8 slices toasted bread
8 tablespoons minced fresh basil
    OR parsley OR chives

Heat the olive oil and butter in a large, heavy skillet over medium-low heat. Add the garlic and sauté the garlic for 5 minutes. Add the wine and pepper and simmer for 15 minutes. Transfer garlic cloves with a slotted spoon to the bowl of a food processor and process until smooth. Reduce cooking liquid by half.

Spread garlic paste on toast and drizzle reduced liquid over garlic. Sprinkle minced herbs over and serve.

Let me die in a tavern so that the wine may be near my dying mouth.

THE ARCHPOET

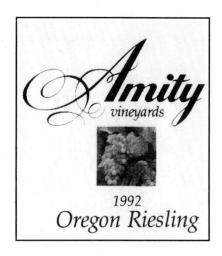

1992
Oregon Riesling

Curried Crab Turnovers

1/2 pound fresh crab meat, picked over
3 tablespoons olive oil
1/2 cup minced onion
3 cloves garlic, minced
1/4 pound mushrooms, chopped
2 stalks celery, finely chopped
2 teaspoons fresh ginger, minced
1 medium tomato, seeded and finely
*   diced*
1/4 cup fresh parsley, minced
2 tablespoons plain yogurt
1/2 teaspoon cumin
1/2 teaspoon salt
1/2 teaspoon turmeric
1/2 teaspoon white pepper
Plain pastry dough, enough for a
*   2-crust pie*
1 egg beaten with 1 tablespoon water

Preheat oven to 375 degrees.

Heat olive oil in a large skillet over medium heat. Add onions and garlic and sauté until they begin to soften. Add the mushrooms, celery and ginger and sauté until the liquid has evaporated and the vegetables are soft but not brown. Remove from the heat and add the crab, tomato, parsley, yogurt, cumin, salt, turmeric and white pepper. Mix well. Set aside to cool.

Roll out the pastry dough and cut into 4-inch rounds. Place 2 tablespoons of the filling in the center of the round. Brush edges with the beaten egg wash, fold over and seal. Place on an ungreased baking sheet. Continue with the remaining filling and pastry until all are used. Brush the tops of the turnovers with egg wash. Bake for about 20 to 25 minutes, or until nicely browned.

Lamb Chops with Plums and Chanterelles

3 tablespoons olive oil
12 lamb chops
32 fresh chanterelle mushrooms
24 yellow plums, pitted
4 tablespoons Brandy
4 cups lamb stock
1 tablespoon German sweet mustard
3 teaspoons minced fresh lemon thyme
*   OR regular thyme*

Heat olive oil in a large, heavy skillet over medium heat. Add the lamb and sauté until nicely browned on both sides. Remove and keep warm.

Add the chanterelles and plums and sauté until mushrooms are cooked, about 4 minutes. Add Brandy and flambé. Add lamb stock, mustard and lemon thyme. Increase heat to medium-high and reduce mixture until thickened. Arrange meat on a platter, pour sauce over meat and serve. Serves 6.

Duck Breast Salad with Pinot Noir Dressing

For the Pinot Noir Dressing:

1/2 cup Pinot Noir
1/2 cup hazelnut oil OR walnut oil
2 tablespoons vegetable oil
1 tablespoon fresh lemon juice
1 teaspoon Dijon mustard
1 teaspoon honey

Combine all ingredients in the bowl of a food processor and process until emulsified. Set aside until needed.

For the Duck Salad:

4 tablespoons butter
2 shallots, minced
1 tablespoon fresh tarragon, minced
6 duck breast halves, skinned and
    boned
Salt and pepper to taste
2 tablespoons butter
6 whole baby zucchini, blossoms
    attached
1 cup orzo pasta
6 cups mixed greens
2 nectarines OR peaches, sliced
6 ounces mild goat cheese, such as
    Montrachet
1/2 cup toasted hazelnuts, coarsely
    chopped
6 edible flowers

Heat butter in a large, heavy skillet over medium-low heat. Add shallots and tarragon and sauté until shallots begin to soften. Add duck breasts and sauté until cooked but still pink in the center, about 4 minutes per side. Remove duck breasts and set aside. Add remaining 2 tablespoons butter to the pan and add zucchini and sauté until tender.

Cook pasta in boiling, salted water until al dente. Drain and toss with 1/2 cup Pinot Noir Dressing.

To assemble the salad, toss the greens with the remaining dressing and divide among 6 plates. Slice duck breasts and fan over the greens. Place zucchini, pasta, nectarine slices and cheese decoratively onto the plates. Garnish with hazelnuts and a flower and serve.

Drunken Fruit over Pound Cake

4 cups mixed fruit such as: peaches,
    nectarines, kiwi fruit, strawberries,
    blueberries or blackberries
1-1/2 cups Amity Vineyards Juliyard
    Vineyards Late Harvest Riesling
1 pound cake OR other dense yellow
    butter cake

Slice fruit in bite-sized pieces if large. Place fruit in a single layer in a glass dish. Pour over Amity Vineyards Juliyard Vineyards Late Harvest Riesling to just cover. Cover and refrigerate at least 2 hours. Serve over pound cake.

When men drink, then they are rich and successful and win lawsuits and are happy and help their friends.

Quickly, bring me a beaker of wine, so that I may wet my mind and say something clever.

ARISTOPHANES

Menu

DINNER ON THE PATIO
for FOUR

Autumn Wind Pinot Gris
**Salmon Galantine
on Baguette Bread**

———

Autumn Wind Sauvignon Blanc
Spiced Shrimp Salad

———

Autumn Wind Chardonnay
**Brie,
Sliced Red and Green Apples
and Assorted Nuts**

———

Autumn Wind Pinot Noir
**Barbecued Pork Tenderloins
with Dried Cherry Chutney**

Garlic Rosemary Potatoes

**Asparagus Tied
with Chives**

———

Autumn Wind Müller-Thurgau
**Fresh Peach Tart
with Almond Crust**

Autumn Wind Vineyard

For us, the decision to name our winery "Autumn Wind" was a natural. We wanted a name that suggests the warmth, the color and the feel of the fall grape harvest in Oregon. As the warm winds blow through the vineyard, and the grape leaves are turned a spectacular gold and red, the newly picked grapes are being wondrously transformed into gold and red wines. This is a time like no other. And it is for this that we are called "Autumn Wind."

Located in the North Chehalem Valley in the heart of Yamhill County's wine country, this 52 acre site was chosen after a long and careful search. The moderate elevation to 450 feet, south sloping exposure, and well-draining soils make it an ideal location for wine grapes. We uprooted old cherry trees and worked hard to clear the land to be able to plant the first vines in 1984. This first planting was predominately a mixture of Chardonnay and various clones of Pinot Noir. In 1990, we added our first planting of Sauvignon Blanc and Pinot Gris.

In 1987, we built Autumn Wind Vineyard Winery. We are currently producing about 6,000 gallons a year, specializing in Pinot Noir, Chardonnay, Pinot Gris, Sauvignon Blanc, and Müller-Thurgau. We feel that by concentrating on fewer varieties, we can put all our efforts into producing truly fine wines. The awards we are winning for these wines have us convinced that this approach is successful.

Having the winery serve as our tasting room allows our visitors to wander among the oak barrels and stainless steel tanks, smelling the wines as they ferment or age and experience a winery first hand. At times, visitors will see a bottling, crushing or pressing as well as getting to taste the grapes as they are picked, or, the juice as it is pressed.

While we have worked long, hard hours, none of this would have been accomplished without our friends. They have volunteered their time and labor in all phases of the winery. They have shared in our efforts and truly know why we fell in love with this business. We hope you will get to share the experience by sampling our wines.

Salmon Galantine

2-1/2 pounds salmon; boned, skinned
    and cubed
5 slices white bread, crusts removed
2 egg whites
1 cup heavy cream
1/2 teaspoon powdered gelatin
1/2 cup chopped fresh herbs (dill,
    chives, basil)
1-1/2 teaspoons salt
1-1/2 teaspoons white pepper

Put all ingredients in the bowl of a food processor and process until smooth. On a large piece of plastic wrap, form salmon mixture into a cylinder, using plastic to help form the roll. Double wrap tightly with plastic wrap and tie both ends securely. Fill a large skillet halfway with water and bring to a simmer over medium-low heat. Place plastic wrapped Galantine in the skillet and poach, turning often, until firm and internal temperature reaches 150 degrees. Remove and cool in ice water. Slice approximately 1/4-inch thick and serve on baguette bread.

Spiced Shrimp Salad

12 large shrimp
1 tablespoon cider vinegar
1/4 teaspoon nutmeg
1/4 teaspoon sugar
1/8 teaspoon mace
Cayenne pepper to taste
5 whole cloves
3 whole allspice berries (optional)
Salad of mixed greens

Put shrimp in a microwave dish. Add vinegar, nutmeg, sugar, mace, cayenne, cloves and allspice and stir gently. Microwave on high for 4 minutes. Turn shrimp and cook for 2 minutes or more if needed. Refrigerate after cooling. Serve on a salad of mixed greens.

Barbecued Pork Tenderloins with Dried Cherry Chutney

For the Pork Tenderloins:

4 pork tenderloins 1-inch thick

Grill pork over medium hot coals for about 20 minutes per side. When done, place on a serving platter and cover with Dried Cherry Chutney. Serves 4.

For the Dried Cherry Chutney:

2 cups dried cherries
1 cup Autumn Wind Pinot Noir
2 shallots, minced
1 tablespoon fresh ginger, minced
2 cloves garlic, minced
2 tablespoons distilled white vinegar
2 tablespoons sugar
1 tablespoon lemon juice
1/2 teaspoon cinnamon

Rehydrate dried cherries in hot water. Drain and chop coarsely. Combine all ingredients in a medium sauce pan and simmer over medium-low heat until shallots and garlic are soft. Remove from heat and let stand for 2 hours before serving, stirring occasionally. Reheat and serve over pork.

Garlic Rosemary Potatoes

4 large red new potatoes
4 cloves garlic, minced
1 sprig fresh rosemary, minced
Olive oil
Salt and pepper to taste

Preheat oven to 375 degrees.

Slice potatoes 1/4-inch thick. Toss with garlic, rosemary, olive oil, salt and pepper until well coated. Spread on a baking sheet with at least 1/2-inch high sides. Bake for 15 minutes, turn over and bake an additional 15 minutes or until done. Serves 4.

Asparagus Tied with Chives

1 pound asparagus
4 long chives

Clean and trim asparagus. Separate into 4 servings and tie with a long chive strand. Lay the bundles in a microwave dish with 1 tablespoon water. Cover and microwave on high for 6 to 8 minutes. Serves 4.

Like the best wine. . . that goeth down sweetly, causing the lips of those that are asleep to speak.

THE BIBLE

Peach Tart with Almond Crust

For the Crust:

1 cup sliced almonds
1 cup flour
1/2 cup sugar
1/2 cup cold butter, cut into pieces
1 egg yolk, beaten
1/2 teaspoon vanilla extract

Preheat oven to 375 degrees.

Place almonds in the bowl of a food processor and process until smooth. Turn off processor and add flour and sugar then add butter. Pulse a few times until mixture resembles coarse meal. Add egg yolk and vanilla and pulse just until mixture forms a ball. Press dough into bottom and sides of a 9-inch tart pan. Prick all over with a fork. Bake for about 20 minutes or until golden brown.

For the Filling:

2 tablespoons peach preserves
1/4 cup sliced almonds, finely chopped
1-1/2 pounds peaches, peeled, pitted and sliced
3 tablespoons sugar
2 tablespoons butter

Spread preserves over cooked tart crust. Sprinkle with 1/4 cup almonds. Arrange peach slices over almonds. Sprinkle sugar over peaches and dot with butter. Bake for 35 minutes.

Menu

A Light Summer Buffet for Ten

Bethel Heights 1992 Chardonnay

Antipasto

Black Bean Dip
with Jicama Dippers

———

Bethel Heights 1992 Pinot Gris

Poached Salmon
with Pear Salsa

Wild Rice and Mussel Salad

Pat's Herb Bread

———

*Bethel Heights 1992 Southeast Block
Pinot Noir*

Pork Loin Marinated
in Pinot Noir

Fresh Green Bean Salad

———

*Bethel Heights 1992
Gewürztraminer*

Chilled Peach Soup

Coffee

Bethel Heights Vineyard

Bethel Heights Vineyard, Inc., was planted in 1977 on a south-facing slope northwest of Salem, Oregon. The vineyard is planted mid-slope on an old lava flow, and the property commands a view of Mount Jefferson as well as Spring Valley. Bethel Heights has earned a national reputation as one of the best vineyard sites in Oregon, particularly for Pinot Noir. Bethel Heights established its reputation as a vineyard of exceptional quality before the first estate wines were produced in 1984. Starting at 3,000 cases, the winery has expanded gradually to 8,500 cases, and at full capacity will produce 10,000 cases of estate bottled wine.

Half of the vineyard, about 23 acres, is planted with Pinot Noir. Several different clones are included, to enhance the complexity of the wines. The fruit is hand-harvested and handled gently throughout the processing to retain its natural flavor and delicacy. About 20% whole clusters (depending on the vintage) go into the tanks first. The rest of the fruit is destemmed, but not crushed. The wine is warm fermented, and remains on the skins in sealed tanks for seven to fourteen days after fermentation, which softens the tannins, adding sweetness and body to the wine. The wines are aged in center-of-France oak for nine to eighteen months, depending on the vintage and the character of specific lots. The wines are racked as little as possible, and are bottled unfiltered.

The winery also produces a variety of excellent white wines, notably Chardonnay, Gewürztraminer and a Vouvray-style Chenin Blanc. New plantings of Pinot Blanc and Pinot Gris will be in production in 1994. As with their Pinot Noir, gentle handling is the rule. Owned and operated by the families of Ted Casteel and Patricia Dudley, and Terry Casteel and Marilyn Webb, one shared focus has been the guiding principle from the beginning: the best wines are produced from the best grapes.

Antipasto

Prepare a variety of summer vegetables for finger food. Here are suggestions, but improvise based on what is fresh.

1 pound pea pods, blanched for
    1 minute and refreshed in
    cold water
1 pound cherry tomatoes
5 stalks celery, cut into 3-inch strips
2 or 3 small zucchini, cut into
    matchsticks
2 red bell peppers, sliced into strips
2 green bell peppers, sliced into strips
Carrot sticks OR baby peeled carrots
Fresh mushrooms, halved
1 15-ounce can artichoke hearts,
    drained and cut into quarters
1/4 pound good quality black
    pitted olives

Prepare vegetables and place in a large container with a lid.

For the Marinade:

2/3 cup white wine vinegar
1/3 cup oil (a small portion of which
    is olive oil)
1/4 cup minced chives OR
    minced red onion OR
    a combination of both
2 cloves garlic, minced
1/2 teaspoon salt
2 tablespoons minced fresh oregano
    OR 1 teaspoon dried oregano
2 tablespoons minced fresh basil
    OR 1 teaspoon dried basil
1/2 teaspoon sugar
Freshly ground pepper to taste

Combine all marinade ingredients in a medium sauce pan and bring to a simmer over medium heat. Remove from heat. Cool for 10 minutes. Pour marinade over prepared vegetables. Cover and refrigerate for 24 hours.

Drain vegetables and arrange decoratively on a serving platter. Provide small plates and forks for those who insist. Serves 10.

14

Black Bean Dip with Jicama Dippers

6 slices bacon, chopped
1/3 cup finely chopped red onion
    OR Walla Walla sweet onion
1/2 teaspoon chili powder
3/4 cup dry black beans, soaked
    overnight and cooked until tender
    (reserve 1/3 cup cooking liquid)
    OR 1 15-ounce can black beans,
    drained with 1/3 cup liquid
    reserved
1 avocado
1/4 cup lemon juice
2 cloves garlic, minced
1 cup shredded Monterey Jack cheese
1/4 cup green onions, minced
1/4 cup minced cilantro
2 red or yellow bell peppers, seeded
    and diced
Cilantro sprigs
2 jicamas
Chili powder

In a large skillet, sauté bacon until crisp. Remove with slotted spoon and drain off all but 1 tablespoon fat. Add onion and chili powder and sauté until tender.

In a large bowl, mash the beans using the reserved liquid as needed to make beans spreadable but not soupy. Add bacon and onion and mix well. Spread this mixture in an 8-inch round on a serving plate.

Peel and mash the avocado with the lemon juice and garlic. Spread avocado mixture over the bean mixture. Top with shredded cheese. Top cheese layer with green onion, cilantro and red peppers. Garnish with cilantro sprigs.

Peel and slice the jicama into 1/4-inch rounds. Cut the rounds into 1/2-inch strips, like thick french fries. Dip one end of the strips lightly into chili powder. Lay the jicama dippers all around the Black Bean Dip, chili end out. Serves 10.

Poached Salmon with Pear Salsa

For the Poached Salmon:

1/2 bottle Bethel Heights Pinot Gris
2 cups water
Juice and zest of 1 lemon
3 cloves garlic, minced
Freshly ground pepper
1 3-pound salmon filet

Preheat oven to 350 degrees.

Choose a roasting pan just large enough to hold the salmon. Pour in Bethel Heights Pinot Gris, water, lemon juice and zest, garlic and pepper. Place pan in oven until mixture begins to simmer. Place salmon in simmering liquid and poach for about 10 minutes or until salmon is firm to the touch. Remove from oven and allow salmon to cool in the poaching liquid. Serve at room temperature with Pear Salsa. Serves 10.

For the Pear Salsa:

6 Oregon pears; peeled, cored and diced
1 tablespoon lemon juice
2 tablespoons oil
1 red onion, julienned
3 cloves garlic, minced
1/3 cup dried cranberries
1/3 cup dried cherries
1-1/2 tablespoons brown sugar
1/4 cup raspberry vinegar
1/2 teaspoon ginger
1/2 teaspoon cardamom
Salt and pepper to taste

Toss diced pears with lemon juice and set aside. Heat oil in a large, heavy skillet over medium heat. Add onion and sauté until they begin to soften. Add garlic and sauté until fragrant. Add pears and sauté until they begin to soften. Drain off any excess liquid. Add dried cranberries, dried cherries and brown sugar, and stir to mix. Stir in vinegar, ginger, cardamom, salt and pepper. Bring to a simmer and simmer for about 5 minutes, stirring constantly. Remove and chill. The Pear Salsa can be made a day in advance. Serve at room temperature.

Good wine
is a good familiar creature
if it be well used.

SHAKESPEARE

Wild Rice and Mussel Salad

This dish can also be made with couscous.

3 pounds fresh mussels, scrubbed, debearded and soaked in cool water for 30 minutes
1 cup water
1/2 cup Bethel Heights Pinot Gris
1 8-ounce box wild rice, cooked according to package directions
1 cup white OR basmati rice, cooked according to package directions
1 small cucumber, peeled, seeded and diced
1/2 teaspoon salt
3 medium tomatoes, seeded and chopped
1 green bell pepper, finely diced
1 cup tiny broccoli florets, steamed until tender but crisp
3/4 cup fresh mixed minced herbs; basil is a must, oregano, thyme, parsley, mint and cilantro are also good
1/4 cup minced green onion
1 tablespoon olive oil
1 tablespoon lemon juice
2 teaspoons minced garlic
1 teaspoon Dijon mustard
1/2 cup toasted hazelnuts, coarsely chopped
Salt and freshly ground pepper
Large lettuce leaves for garnish

Combine water and Bethel Heights Pinot Gris in a large pot. Bring to a simmer over medium-high heat. Add mussels and shake to coat with broth. Cover tightly and let steam for 3 minutes. Shake pan again, without lifting lid, and continue steaming for an additional 3 minutes. Discard any mussels that did not open. Remove meat from shells and chop coarsely, reserve. Bring broth to a boil and reduce to 1/2 cup. Strain reduced broth through cheesecloth, and reserve. This can be done earlier in the day and refrigerated separately.

Combine cooked wild rice and cooked white rice in a large bowl. Add as much reserved broth as rice will take, it should be moist but not soggy. Set aside.

Sprinkle diced cucumber with salt and let stand for 20 minutes. Rinse and pat dry. Add to rice mixture with tomatoes, green pepper, broccoli, fresh herbs and green onion.

In a small bowl, whisk together olive oil, lemon juice, garlic, and Dijon mustard until smooth. Pour over salad and toss well. Add reserved chopped mussels and hazelnuts and toss well. Add salt and pepper to taste. Chill for 1 to 4 hours before serving to allow flavors to marry. Line a large serving bowl with lettuce leaves and place Wild Rice and Mussel Salad on lettuce. Serves 10.

Pat's Herb Bread

Parsley and chives will take over your garden if you let them. Here is a good way to use a lot of both. This recipe makes 2 fat baguettes. It will serve 10 people modestly, but to have plenty with leftovers to toast later, you might want to double the recipe.

2 tablespoons yeast
2 teaspoons sugar
1/2 cup warm water (100 degrees to 115 degrees)
1 cup coarse cornmeal
1 cup fresh parsley leaves, chopped
3/4 cup chopped chives
3 tablespoons olive oil
2 teaspoons salt
1/8 teaspoon cayenne
1-1/2 cups hot water
2 eggs, beaten
2 cups whole wheat flour
1/2 cup soy flour
1/2 cup toasted sesame seeds
2 cups unbleached white flour plus 1/2 cup more if needed
Cornmeal for the baking sheet

Preheat oven to 375 degrees. Lightly grease a baking sheet and sprinkle with cornmeal.

Dissolve yeast and sugar in 1/2 cup warm water and set aside until it starts foaming.

Place cornmeal, parsley, chives, olive oil, salt and cayenne in a large bowl. Add the 1-1/2 cups hot water and stir. Set aside to cool.

When cornmeal mixture is cool, stir in yeast mixture, eggs, whole wheat flour, soy flour and sesame seeds. Gradually add the white flour until the dough is easy to handle. Turn dough out onto a lightly floured board and knead until smooth and elastic, add more flour as needed to keep dough from sticking. Place dough in an oiled bowl and turn to coat on all sides. Cover with a damp towel and let rise in a warm place until doubled in bulk, about 1-1/2 hours.

Punch down dough and divide into 2 equal parts. Roll out each portion into a rectangle about 12-inches by 8-inches. Beginning with the long side, roll up dough tightly and pinch to seal. Place seam side down on prepared baking sheet, spaced well apart. Make 1/4-inch slashes diagonally across the top of loaf at 1/2-inch intervals OR 1 slash lengthwise. Let rise until doubled in bulk, about 1 hour. Bake for about 25 to 30 minutes, or until golden brown. Let cool on rack for 10 minutes before slicing.

Forsake not an old friend;
for the new is not comparable to him:
a new friend is as new wine;
when it is old, it is drunk with pleasure.

THE BIBLE

Pork Loin Marinated in Pinot Noir

For the Marinade:

2 tablespoons olive oil
5 medium carrots, coarsely chopped
1 large onion, coarsely chopped
3 cloves garlic, minced
5 cups Bethel Heights First Release
    Pinot Noir
1/2 cup raspberry vinegar
1/4 cup fresh parsley, coarsely chopped
4 bay leaves
15 juniper berries
10 black peppercorns
1 teaspoon salt

Heat oil in a large skillet over medium heat and add carrots, onion, and garlic and sauté until lightly browned. Add Bethel Heights First Release Pinot Noir, raspberry vinegar, parsley, bay leaves, juniper berries, peppercorns and salt and simmer for 10 minutes. Cool. Put marinade in a non-reactive bowl and place meat in marinade. Cover and refrigerate for two or three days, turning occasionally.

For the Mustard Coating:

1 cup Dijon mustard
1/3 cup chopped onion
1/4 cup Bethel Heights Chardonnay
1/4 cup olive oil
3 large cloves garlic, coarsely chopped
1 teaspoon minced fresh sage
    OR 1/2 teaspoon dried sage
1 teaspoon minced fresh thyme
    OR 1/2 teaspoon dried thyme
1 teaspoon salt
Freshly ground pepper to taste

Place all ingredients in the bowl of a food processor and process until smooth.

For the Pork Loin:

5 to 6 pounds boneless center-cut
    loin of pork, well trimmed

Preheat oven to 400 degrees.

Remove meat from marinade and pat dry. Heat a little oil in a sauté pan over medium heat. Sear meat on all sides. If necessary, do this in batches. Place on rack in a roasting pan. Coat pork with Mustard Coating. Bake for about 35 to 45 minutes or until meat thermometer reads 160 degrees. Remove from oven and let pork rest for 10 minutes before carving. Serves 10.

It is better to hide ignorance,
but it is hard to do when we relax over wine.

HERACLITUS

Fresh Green Bean Salad

2 pounds fresh young green beans,
    ends snipped
1 small onion, finely chopped
2/3 cup olive oil
2/3 cup freshly grated Parmesan cheese
1/4 cup white wine vinegar
3 tablespoons minced fresh basil
    OR tarragon
2 cloves garlic, minced
3/4 teaspoon salt
Freshly ground pepper to taste
2 tomatoes, seeded and diced

Cook beans in boiling water until just tender. Plunge in cold water to cool. Drain well. Combine onion, olive oil, Parmesan, vinegar, basil, garlic, salt and pepper in an attractive serving bowl. Add beans and toss well. Scatter tomatoes over the top. Serve at room temperature. Serves 10.

BETHEL HEIGHTS VINEYARD

OREGON CHENIN BLANC

WILLAMETTE VALLEY

1993   ALCOHOL 13.0% BY VOLUME

Chilled Peach Soup

This works very well for a buffet-style, informal meal. I serve it in my ceramic bread bowl, with cups or mugs close by for self-serve. Spoons on the side and a bowl of light sour cream for those who want a dollop. Scatter mint sprigs around the outside of the bowl for garnish.

25 Oregon fresh, ripe peaches, peeled
    and cut into chunks
2 cups freshly squeezed orange juice
3/4 cup pineapple chunks, in their
    own juice, drained and
    reserve juice
2 teaspoons ground ginger
2 tablespoons powdered sugar
1/2 cup light sour cream (optional)
Additional light sour cream for
    garnish

Puree peaches in food processor with a little of the orange juice. Do this in batches until all is processed. Pour into a large serving bowl. Puree pineapple and add to peach mixture. Stir in remaining orange juice and pineapple juice. Add ginger and powdered sugar. Stir to blend well. Stir in 1/2 cup sour cream. Chill at least 6 hours before serving. Serve with a bowl of additional sour cream. Serves 10.

Menu

BASTILLE DAY BUFFET
À LA PROVENCE

Chateau Benoit Pinot Gris
Marinated Shrimp

———

Chateau Benoit Sauvignon Blanc
Tomato, Goat Cheese
and Basil Salad
with Balsamic Vinaigrette

———

Chateau Benoit Pinot Noir
Oregon Leg of Lamb
with Tarragon
and Red Potatoes

Mold of Eggplant

———

Chateau Benoit Sweet Marie
Tri-Color Cream Tart
with Sweet Marie

———

A finale—a glass of
Chateau Benoit Sparkling Brut.
Let's toast to freedom
for all people everywhere!
Salut!

Chateau Benoit Winery

In 1972, Fred Benoit realized the beginning of a long cherished dream when he and Mary Benoit bought land near Veneta, Oregon, and planted their first vineyard. A full time medical practice allowed little time for this venture, but with the help of friends and their three sons, 22 acres of Pinot Noir, Chardonnay and Riesling were planted.

Believing that the star area of the Oregon wine industry would prove to be Yamhill County, Fred left his medical practice in 1979, and the couple moved 100 miles north to Lafayette, where they founded the winery and planted a new vineyard. The original vineyard has since been sold.

For ten years wine making, bottling, aging and sales all took place in one large space. Then, in 1989, the Benoits and their new partner, Bill Wittenberg, were able to secure financing to complete the chateau, which is now pictured on the label. The large hospitality room and patio overlooking lush countryside and the Coast Range have drawn thousands of visitors to the winery each year. The hospitality area has become a popular site for weddings, dinners and gatherings of all kinds.

Although Fred and Mary grew up in Yakima, Washington, and have lived in many parts of the United States, they are both descendants of historic Oregon pioneer families. Their six grown children and five grandchildren are all currently living in the Northwest. The ice wine, Sweet Marie, is named for the first granddaughter.

Annual production is 15,000 to 18,000 cases. A wide variety of wines are made, with Sauvignon Blanc and Pinot Noir the house favorites and Müller-Thurgau the public favorite. They also make Chardonnay, Brut Sparkling, Pinot Gris, Dry White Riesling, Dry Gewürztraminer, Merlot, and Sweet Marie Ice Wine.

Ardent Francophiles, the Benoits travel to Europe as often as circumstances allow. A week spent in Provence in 1993 prompted the theme for this menu. Bon Appétit!

Marinated Shrimp

*3 pounds large raw shrimp (15 to 20
    to the pound)*
1/2 cup olive oil
1/2 cup bread crumbs, toasted
1/2 cup freshly grated Parmesan cheese
2 cloves garlic, crushed
1/2 cup olive oil
3 tablespoons lemon juice
Salt and freshly ground pepper
2 tablespoons minced fresh parsley

Split shrimp lengthwise but leave in the shells. Mix 1/2 cup olive oil, bread crumbs, Parmesan and garlic. Spread over the cut surface of shrimp. Place on rack of broiler pan and broil until brown, about 2 to 4 minutes.

Arrange shrimp on serving platter. Combine remaining 1/2 cup olive oil, lemon juice, salt and pepper. Spoon over shrimp and let stand until cool. Cover and chill in refrigerator for at least 1 hour and up to 24 hours. Bring to room temperature, sprinkle with parsley and serve. Serves 8.

To be crushed in the winepress of passion.

GABRIEL BIEL

Tomato, Goat Cheese and Basil Salad with Balsamic Vinaigrette

4 fully ripe large tomatoes
*2 8-ounce logs Montrachet
    OR domestic goat cheese*
Lettuce leaves
1 bunch fresh basil leaves

For the Balsamic Vinaigrette:

1/4 cup extra virgin olive oil
*1 to 2 tablespoons Balsamic vinegar,
    to taste*
Salt and pepper to taste

Cut tomatoes and goat cheese into uniform slices. Alternate on serving plate on a bed of lettuce leaves. Garnish with basil leaves.

Combine Balsamic Vinaigrette ingredients in a jar with a lid and shake to emulsify. Drizzle over salad and serve. Serves 8.

Oregon Leg of Lamb with Tarragon and Red Potatoes

1 7 to 8 pound leg of lamb
2 cloves garlic, peeled and cut into
    slivers
Salt and pepper
2 tablespoons minced fresh tarragon
    leaves
2 tablespoons olive oil
16 to 20 tiny red potatoes
1/2 cup Chateau Benoit Pinot Noir

Preheat oven to 375 degrees.

Trim outer skin and excess fat from lamb. Make several incisions with a small knife and insert garlic slivers. Rub meat with salt, pepper, tarragon then with olive oil. Place lamb in roasting pan then roast in oven about 15 to 20 minutes per pound or until meat thermometer reads 160 degrees. About 45 minutes before lamb is done, scrub potatoes, rub with additional olive oil and place in pan around meat in roasting pan. Turn potatoes occasionally to brown all over. Remove meat and potatoes to serving platter and allow meat to rest for 15 minutes before carving.

Remove excess fat from roasting pan and discard fat. Place pan on top of stove over medium heat. When hot, add Chateau Benoit Pinot Noir and whisk to deglaze pan, making sure to whisk up any browned bits.

Slice lamb and pour pan juices over lamb and potatoes. Serves 8.

Mold of Eggplant

3 to 4 small eggplants (about 2-1/2
    pounds), stems discarded, cut
    into 3/8-inch slices
Salt
2 tablespoons olive oil
1 medium onion, finely chopped
1 clove garlic, minced
4 cups Italian-style canned plum
    tomatoes, drained and chopped
Salt and freshly ground pepper to taste
1/2 cup olive oil
1 cup plain yogurt
1/2 cup chicken stock

Preheat oven to 350 degrees.

Sprinkle eggplant slices with salt and place in a colander in the sink. Let drain for 30 minutes. Rinse in cold water and dry on paper towels.

Heat 2 tablespoons olive oil in a large skillet over medium heat. Add onion and sauté until lightly browned. Add garlic and sauté until fragrant. Add tomatoes, salt and pepper and simmer, stirring occasionally until mixture is thick and pulpy, about 20 to 25 minutes. Remove 1/3 of tomato sauce and set aside.

Heat 1/2 cup olive oil in a large skillet and brown eggplant slices on both sides. Place one slice in the bottom of a 2-quart charlotte mold or other mold. Halve remaining slices. Begin arranging slices in overlapping concentric circles. Spread with a little tomato sauce and yogurt. Continue layering until all ingredients have been used, ending with eggplant layer. Cover with foil and bake for about 40 to 50 minutes, or until eggplant is very tender. Let cool completely in mold.

Combine reserved tomato sauce and chicken stock in a small sauce pan. Bring to a simmer over medium heat, whisking constantly, for 2 to 3 minutes. Remove from heat and let cool to room temperature. To serve, unmold eggplant onto platter and spoon sauce around the base. Serves 8.

Tri-Color Cream Tart with Sweet Marie

For the Pastry:

*1/2 cup unsalted butter, at room
    temperature
1/3 cup sugar
1/2 teaspoon vanilla extract
1/4 teaspoon salt
1-1/4 cups flour*

Preheat oven to 375 degrees. Butter a 10-inch fluted tart pan with a removable bottom.

In a medium bowl, cream together butter, sugar, vanilla and salt with an electric mixer. Add flour and blend until mixture forms crumbs that becomes dough when pressed together. Turn dough into prepared tart pan and press firm and evenly into the bottom and sides of the pan. Chill the pastry for 30 minutes.

Prick the pastry all over with a fork, line it with foil and fill with pie weights or raw rice. Bake in lower 1/3 of oven for 15 minutes. Remove weights and foil and bake an additional 10 minutes or until golden. Cool on rack for 5 minutes, remove side of pan and cool completely. The pastry shell will be very crisp.

For the Cream:

*3 large egg yolks
1/2 cup sugar
3 tablespoons cornstarch
1 teaspoon vanilla extract
3/4 cup milk
1/4 cup Chateau Benoit Sweet Marie
    Ice Wine
1/2 cup heavy cream, chilled*

In a medium sauce pan, whisk together the egg yolks, sugar, cornstarch and vanilla until smooth. Whisk in milk. Place over medium heat and bring to a simmer, whisking constantly. Simmer for about 3 minutes, whisking constantly, or until very thick. Take care not to let mixture scorch. Transfer to a bowl and slowly whisk in Chateau Benoit Sweet Marie Ice Wine. Cover with plastic wrap and chill 4 hours or until firm.

In a different chilled bowl, whip heavy cream until it holds stiff peaks. Whisk previously prepared cream mixture until smooth then whisk in half the whipped heavy cream to lighten mixture. Fold in remaining half of whipped cream gently.

For the Topping:

*1 quart whole strawberries, hulled
2 cups blueberries
1 cup raspberries*

Place pastry shell on a serving plate and fill with Cream. Stand strawberries, hulled side down, in the Cream. Scatter other berries over and between strawberries. Chill tart for 1 to 6 hours before serving. Serves 8.

CHATEAU BENOIT

1991

Sweet Marie

PRODUCED AND BOTTLED BY CHATEAU BENOIT CARLTON, OREGON.
375 ML. CONTAINS SULFITES. ALCOHOL 12.5% BY VOLUME.

If all be true that I do think,
There are five reasons we should drink:
Good wine—a friend—or being dry—
Or lest we should be by and by—
Or any other reason why.

HENRY ALDRICH

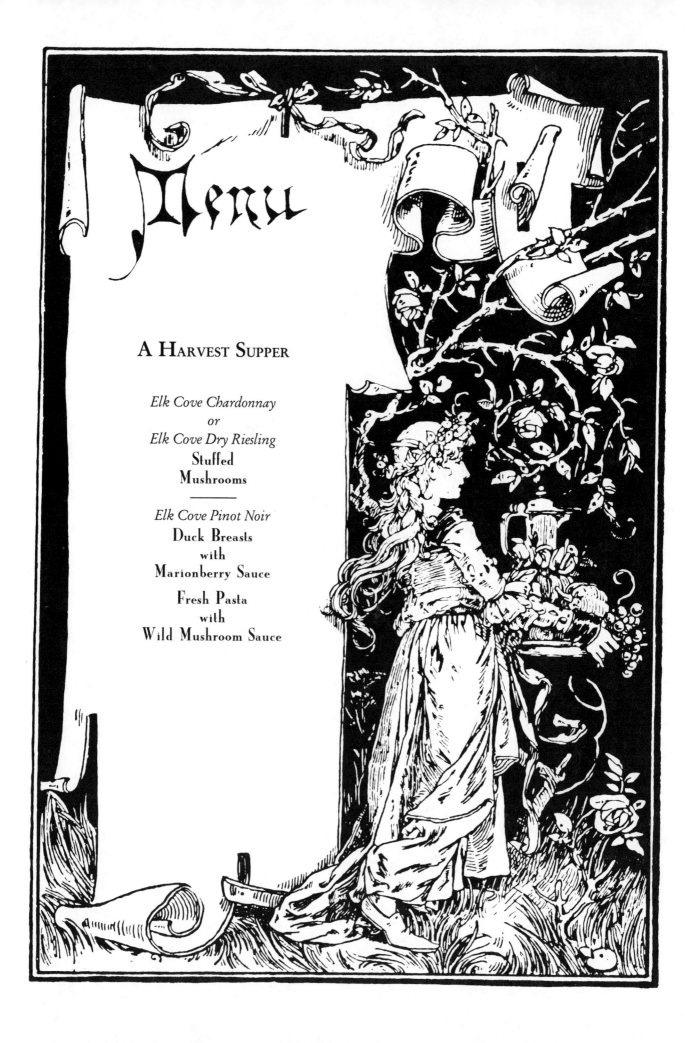

Menu

A Harvest Supper

Elk Cove Chardonnay
or
Elk Cove Dry Riesling
Stuffed
Mushrooms

———

Elk Cove Pinot Noir
Duck Breasts
with
Marionberry Sauce

Fresh Pasta
with
Wild Mushroom Sauce

Elk Cove Vineyards

After a lengthy search in Northern Oregon for the perfect location, Pat and Joe Campbell founded Elk Cove Vineyards with the planting of their first 10 acres of grapes in 1974. The soil type, drainage and unique micro-climate of this small, protected valley have indeed proven it to be one of Oregon's outstanding sites for the growing of cool climate varieties. The Campbells have planted Pinot Noir, Chardonnay, Pinot Gris, Riesling, and Gewürztraminer.

After four years of production in a renovated farm building, the winery and tasting room were built in 1981 on a small plateau in the middle of their 45 acres of vineyard. This location was chosen for the proximity to the vines and the beauty of the setting.

Twenty additional acres will be planted in the remaining farmable land. The other 80 acres will remain as is, in a steep canyon of Douglas firs, Oregon White Oak and Big Leaf Maple.

The production of the winery is now at 12,000 cases and will peak at 15,000. Small is indeed beautiful and the geography of the hillside land in the Northern Willamette helps insure this atmosphere.

Joe and Pat Campbell have each brought varied backgrounds to Elk Cove Vineyards. Pat, as general manager and assistant winemaker, benefitted greatly from her Swiss farming background. After emigrating from Switzerland her great-grandfather planted a vineyard of Chasselas in the late 1880's in Helvetia, Oregon. There he made and sold wine to the community.

Her father and mother grew pears and apples in the Hood River Valley where Pat grew up before leaving to study French and German at the University of Oregon. She brings to the winery a solid viticulture background, an accomplished palate, and good organizational skills.

Joe, the winemaker, was also raised in Hood River. He studied History of Science at Harvard and medicine at Stanford where he and Pat first became enamored of wine growing. He brings a strong element of caution and care to winemaking. The Hippocratic oath, "First do no harm" is a credo in his winemaking and viticulture as well as in his medical practice. Natural products for the fining and clarifying of wine-gelatin, Bentonite clay, egg whites, small amounts of sulfur, and cultured yeasts are the only additions. The wines are handled gently from the crushing to the bottling.

Joe still practices medicine three days a week, except during the month of harvest.

These are some of our favorite recipes for a late summer or early autumn meal. Serve with a fresh green salad with a light vinaigrette, good bread and a fruit tart for dessert. Great for harvest appetites.

Stuffed Mushrooms

2 pounds large mushrooms
8 tablespoons butter
1/2 cup fresh shiitaki mushrooms
    OR 1/4 cup dried shiitaki
    mushrooms rehydrated, chopped
1/4 cup shallots, finely chopped
2 tablespoons brandy
2 tablespoons flour
1/4 cup Elk Cove Chardonnay
1/4 cup cream
Cayenne pepper to taste
Salt to taste
1/4 pound Gruyère cheese, grated

Preheat oven to 350 degrees.

Clean and dry the mushrooms and remove the caps. Heat 2 tablespoons of the butter in a sauté pan over medium heat. Add the mushroom caps and sauté until just tender. Remove and set aside.

Chop the mushroom stems. Heat 4 tablespoons of the butter in the sauté pan over medium heat. Add the chopped mushroom stems, shiitaki mushrooms and shallots. Sauté until tender. Add brandy and flame immediately. Remove from pan and set aside.

Melt remaining 2 tablespoons butter in the pan over medium-low heat. Whisk in the flour to make a roux. Whisk in the wine and simmer, whisking constantly, until sauce has thickened, about 4 minutes. Whisk in cream, cayenne pepper and salt. Blend in chopped mushroom mixture.

Place a spoonful of mushroom mixture into mushroom caps. Cover with grated Gruyère cheese. Bake until cheese has melted, about 10 minutes. Serve immediately.

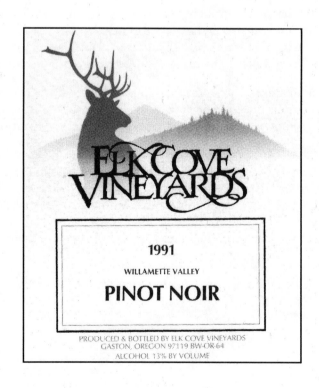

ELK COVE VINEYARDS

1991

WILLAMETTE VALLEY

PINOT NOIR

PRODUCED & BOTTLED BY ELK COVE VINEYARDS
GASTON, OREGON 97119 BW-OR-64
ALCOHOL 13% BY VOLUME

Duck Breasts with Marionberry Sauce

8 boned duck breasts

Preheat oven to 400 degrees.

Place duck breasts skin side up in a roasting pan just large enough to hold them. Roast for about 1 hour.

For the Sauce:

4 cups excellent veal or duck stock
1/2 cup Elk Cove Chardonnay
Salt and pepper to taste
2 tablespoons arrowroot
*   OR cornstarch*
2 tablespoons cold water
1/2 cup marionberry preserves
*   (not too sweet)*
2 tablespoons red wine vinegar
1/2 cup fresh raspberries

Place stock and wine in a sauce pan and cook over medium heat until mixture has reduced to 2 cups. Season with salt and pepper. Set aside.

Broil tops of the duck breasts until crisp and brown. Remove duck to a platter and keep warm. Remove all but 1 tablespoon of grease from the roasting pan. Place pan on stove over medium heat. When hot, add stock and Elk Cove Chardonnay and deglaze pan, whisking up any browned bits. Dissolve arrowroot in cold water and whisk into pan. Simmer until slightly thickened, about 2 minutes.

Whisk together preserves and vinegar in a small sauce pan and cook over medium-low heat until blended and thickened, about 2 minutes, stirring constantly. Set aside.

Pour sauce onto plates, place a duck breast on the sauce and top with 1/2 tablespoon of marionberry mixture on the breast. Garnish with raspberries.

Fresh Pasta with Wild Mushroom Sauce

1/2 cup dried morel or boletus
*   mushrooms*
1/2 cup hot water
1/4 cup dry sherry OR dry Marsala
*   wine*
3 tablespoons butter
3 tablespoons flour
1 cup cream
White pepper to taste
Nutmeg to taste
1 pound fresh angel hair pasta

Soak dried mushrooms in water and sherry for 15 minutes. Melt butter in a saucepan over low heat. Whisk in flour to make a roux and cook for 4 minutes, whisking constantly. Slowly whisk in liquid from mushrooms and cream. Sauce should not be too thick. Season with white pepper and nutmeg, then stir in mushrooms.

Cook pasta in boiling water until al dente. Toss with Wild Mushroom Sauce and serve immediately.

Menu

An Autumn Dinner

Eyrie Vineyards Pinot Gris
Smoked Salmon Spread

———

Eyrie Vineyards Pinot Noir
Roasted Chicken
with
Herbed Ricotta Stuffing

Wild Rice

Steamed Carrots

———

Hazelnut Shortbread
with
Oregon Fruit Compote

The Eyrie Vineyards

The Eyrie Vineyards was established by David and Diana Lett in 1966. It was the first vinifera (European winegrape) vineyard to be planted in the Willamette Valley of western Oregon since Prohibition, and pioneered the present-day premium wine industry of this region. The 46-acre vineyard is located in the Red Hills of Dundee, about 30 miles southwest of the city of Portland. It was named for the red-tailed hawks who have made their home (eye-rie) in the fir trees at the top of the vineyard.

David Lett received his education in grape growing and winemaking at the University of California at Davis, where he became particularly interested in the wine variety Pinot Noir. After graduation in 1964, he spent almost a year in the winegrowing regions of northern Europe, researching the climatic requirements of Pinot Noir. This research convinced him that the most suitable American climate for Pinot Noir was not to be found in California, but further north, in the cooler, much more "marginal" climate of the Willamette Valley.

In 1979, in the "Olympiades of the Wines of the World" held in Paris, and in the subsequent Drouhin Tasting held in Burgundy in 1980, the Eyrie Vineyards 1975 Pinot Noir became the first American Pinot Noir to successfully compete against the renowned Pinot Noirs of France.

In addition to hand-crafted Pinot Noir and Chardonnay, The Eyrie Vineyards also produces Pinot Gris, Pinot Meunier, and a dry Muscat Ottonel. The original 20 acres also contained small experimental plantings of these three unusual wine varieties. The popularity of Pinot Gris, and the excellence of its performance in the climate of the northern Willamette Valley, encouraged the Letts to commit 26 additional acres to this variety. Other winegrowers are also planting Pinot Gris now, and it promises to become, along with Pinot Noir, one of Oregon's most distinctive wine varieties.

The Eyrie Vineyards is quite small, with a total annual production of only 5,000 to 7,000 cases. Because production is so limited, there is no "tasting room" as such at the winery in McMinnville. However, the Letts host an annual "Thanksgiving Weekend Winetasting" of their newest releases, and private visits for small groups may be arranged throughout the year by appointment.

Smoked Salmon Spread

This recipe is from Billie Sutton who has hand-labeled every bottle of wine since our first vintage in 1970. She also worked in the vineyard from 1967 to 1982.

1-1/2 cups smoked salmon (boned and skinned), flaked
8 ounces cream cheese, softened
3 teaspoons prepared horseradish
3 green onions, finely chopped
1/4 cup chopped walnuts
Fresh parsley

Mix salmon, cream cheese, horseradish and green onions together until smooth. Shape into a ball (it will be soft), and roll in chopped walnuts. Gently press into a metal bowl to shape, then invert onto a plate to serve. Garnish with parsley. Serve at room temperature with a variety of crackers or sliced French bread.

In vino veritas.

(In wine is truth.)

Roasted Chicken with Herbed Ricotta Stuffing

1 2-1/2-pound roasting chicken
Salt and pepper
5 tablespoons minced fresh parsley
2 green onions, tops included, minced
1 clove garlic, minced
2 teaspoons minced fresh tarragon
1/4 teaspoon minced fresh oregano
1/4 teaspoon minced fresh thyme
1 tablespoon ricotta cheese
1 teaspoon oil
3/4 cup chicken stock

Preheat oven to 425 degrees.

Season chicken inside and out with salt and pepper. With your fingers (don't use a knife), working from the neck opening down, gently separate the skin from the breast meat, on down to the tops of the drumsticks.

Combine parsley, green onions, garlic, tarragon, oregano, thyme and ricotta and make a paste with a mortar and pestle. Spread this mixture as evenly as possible on the breast and thigh meat underneath the skin. Pat the skin back in place and truss the chicken. Brush the skin lightly with 1 teaspoon oil.

Roast the chicken at 425 for 20 minutes. Reduce oven to 350 degrees and continue roasting for an additional 40 minutes, or until the chicken is nicely browned and the juices run clear when pierced.

Remove chicken to a warm platter and keep warm. Remove excess fat from roasting pan. Place pan on stove over medium-high heat. Whisk in chicken stock, scraping up any browned bits. Continue to cook until reduced by half.

Cut the chicken into serving pieces and place on platter. Pour the stock reduction over the chicken and garnish with parsley. Serves 4.

Wild Rice

4 cups chicken stock
1-1/2 cups wild rice
1 teaspoon salt

Bring chicken stock to a boil in a medium sauce pan. Stir in rice and salt with a fork. Reduce heat to low, cover and simmer for about 35 minutes or until liquid is absorbed. Serves 4.

Hazelnut Shortbread with Oregon Fruit Compote

1/2 cup butter
1/2 cup shortening
1/3 cup sugar
1 teaspoon vanilla extract
1/4 teaspoon almond extract
2-1/4 cups flour
1/4 cup ground toasted hazelnuts
1/8 teaspoon salt

Preheat oven to 325 degrees.

In a large bowl, cream together butter, shortening, sugar, vanilla extract and almond extract until smooth. Stir in flour, hazelnuts and salt. Press dough into an ungreased 9-inch by 13-inch pan. Bake for 50 minutes, or until lightly golden. Let cool completely before cutting into serving pieces. Serve with Oregon Fruit Compote.

Oregon Fruit Compote:

Peaches
Strawberries
Blueberries
Raspberries
Blackberries
Sugar
Cointreau

About an hour before dinnertime, slice peaches, strawberries, blueberries, raspberries and blackberries into a pretty glass bowl. Add sugar to taste and stir in about 2 tablespoons Cointreau. Let sit until time for dessert.

Menu

AFTER THE GAME DINNER

Golden Valley Golden Ale
**Golden Valley
Crab Cakes
with Rémoulade Sauce**

Golden Valley Red Thistle Ale
**Sliced Red Onion and
Cucumber Salad
with Citrus Vinaigrette**

**Fresh Focaccia with
Pesto**

Golden Valley Pinot Noir
**Tuscan
Grilled Chicken**

**Garlic
Smashed Potatoes**

**Yellow and Green Zucchini
with
Sweet Red Pepper
and Thyme**

**Fresh Oregon Blackberry
and Apple Cobbler**

Golden Valley Vineyards

Golden Valley Vineyards produced its first vintage Pinot Noir in 1992, using grapes grown in the owner's vineyard, Saint Herman's Vineyard, located in the Red Hills south of Dundee, Oregon. Saint Herman was the patron saint of Kodiak Island in Alaska, where Peter and Celia Kircher lived for twelve years and operated their commercial fishing boat. In 1987, they sold their home in Kodiak and moved to the Northwest in search of a farm to raise their family.

After tasting an Adelsheim 1983 Pinot Noir in 1987, the Kirchers were convinced that Oregon had the potential to produce wine of world class quality and began their search for a suitable vineyard site. Almost a year later, after looking at one vineyard site, they by chance heard of another possible site in the Red Hills and went to see it in the fog and pouring rain. They bought it that day and Peter left for three months salmon fishing season in Alaska the next day.

Saint Herman's Vineyard is an ideal location at the higher elevation of the Red Hills, direct southern exposure with good wind protection, and adjacent to Domaine Drouhin, Domain Serene, Eyrie and Sokol Blosser Vineyards. At present, the vineyard is planted with 15 acres of Pinot Noir, Pommard and Wadensville clones, and 5 acres of Dijon clone Chardonnays.

In 1992, the Kirchers began to see a serious decline in the fishing market in Alaska. The supply was still strong but the market was controlled by foreign interests and farm raised fish were putting a serious strain on the market. In looking for a new business venture to undertake in conjunction with the vineyard, the microbrew industry took their attention and in December of 1993 they opened Golden Valley Brewery & Pub in downtown McMinnville, in the heart of Oregon wine country.

Golden Valley Brewery & Pub produces six traditional style ales consisting of an American Wheat beer, Golden Ale, Amber Ale, Porter Ale and our Red Thistle Ale. Both the Porter Ale and the Red Thistle Ale are kegged and sold at other pubs in Portland and outlying areas. We believe that quality should be at the foundation of any product, and we carry this philosophy through our brewery, kitchen and winemaking. All of our foods, beers and wines are handmade with the finest ingredients available, buying locally produced foods from the abundant Willamette Valley and seafood from the Pacific Northwest whenever possible.

Golden Valley Crab Cakes with Rémoulade Sauce

For the Crab Cakes:

12 ounces fresh Oregon crab meat,
    picked over for shells
1/2 cup Panko bread crumbs
    OR other plain bread crumbs
1/4 cup finely chopped celery
1/4 cup finely chopped green onions
1/4 cup finely chopped red bell pepper
1/4 cup mayonnaise
2 teaspoons lemon juice
2 teaspoons Worcestershire sauce
1 teaspoon dry mustard
1 teaspoon Tabasco sauce
1 to 4 cloves garlic, minced
Melted butter
Panko bread crumbs OR other
    plain bread crumbs for breading
Lemon wedges

In a large bowl combine crab, 1/2 cup bread crumbs, celery, green onions, bell pepper, mayonnaise, lemon juice, Worcestershire sauce, mustard, Tabasco and garlic and mix well. Form mixture into small cakes. Dip in melted butter, then in bread crumbs. Chill. Heat butter in a sauté pan over medium-low heat. Sauté Crab Cakes until golden on both sides. Serve with lemon wedges and Rémoulade Sauce. Serves 6.

For the Rémoulade Sauce:

1 cup mayonnaise
1/3 cup finely chopped Kosher dill
    pickles
2 tablespoons capers
1 tablespoon Dijon mustard
1 tablespoon minced parsley
1 tablespoon white wine
2 teaspoons anchovy paste
1 teaspoon Tabasco sauce
1/8 teaspoon tarragon
1/8 teaspoon chervil

Combine all ingredients and mix well. Cover and chill overnight before serving.

Sliced Red Onion and Cucumber Salad with Citrus Vinaigrette

6 cups Mescal mixed lettuce OR butter
    lettuce and red leaf lettuce mixed
Juice and zest of 1 orange
Juice and zest of 1 lemon
Juice and zest of 1 lime
1/4 cup honey
1/2 cup olive oil
1 large cucumber, halved lengthwise,
    seeded and sliced
1 large red onion, thinly sliced
Mint leaves for garnish

Wash lettuce mix in warm water, drain well and store in a bowl covered with a damp paper towel in the refrigerator.

Whisk together orange juice and zest, lemon juice and zest, lime juice and zest, honey and olive oil in a medium bowl. Place cucumber and onion in Citrus Vinaigrette and toss well. Cover and refrigerate for 30 minutes before serving.

Line 6 plates with 1 cup lettuce mix, spoon onion and cucumber on top and drizzle with Vinaigrette. Garnish with mint leaves. Serves 6.

Fresh Focaccia with Pesto

Cornmeal for the baking sheet
1/4 cup lukewarm water
1 package yeast
1 teaspoon sugar
2 cups flour
1/2 cup warm water
3 tablespoons cornmeal
3 tablespoons olive oil
1/2 cup pesto
3 tablespoons olive oil

Preheat oven to 375 degrees. Sprinkle cornmeal on a baking sheet.

In a large bowl, combine 1/4 cup water, yeast and sugar and allow to proof for 5 minutes. Add flour, 1 cup water, 3 tablespoons cornmeal and 3 tablespoons olive oil and stir until stiff. Turn out dough onto a lightly floured board and knead until smooth and elastic. Place dough in a lightly oiled bowl and turn to coat. Cover and let raise in a warm place until doubled in bulk.

Stretch dough out evenly on baking sheet and allow to raise again for 1 hour. Make indentations with finger every three inches. Bake for about 15 minutes then remove from oven and spread pesto gently on top of dough. Drizzle 3 tablespoons olive oil over top. Bake for an additional 10 to 15 minutes or until golden brown. Cool on a rack and cut into squares.

Tuscan Grilled Chicken

2 3-pound whole Oregon fryer
chickens

Preheat oven to 350 degrees.

Split chickens in half lengthwise, cut away backbone and reserve for making stock.

For the Marinade:

2 cups olive oil
1 small yellow onion, thinly sliced
Juice of 1 lemon
1 sprig fresh rosemary
OR 2 tablespoons dry rosemary
3 cloves garlic, minced
1 tablespoon salt
1 tablespoon pepper
1 bay leaf
1 teaspoon red chili flakes

Whisk together marinade ingredients in a shallow dish. Place chickens in marinade and turn to coat well. Cover and refrigerate overnight, turning occasionally.

Place chickens in a roasting pan and roast for about 45 minutes, or until internal temperature reaches 175 degrees. Serves 6.

Garlic Smashed Potatoes

2 pounds red potatoes, peeled
7 to 9 cloves garlic, peeled
2/3 cup sour cream
6 tablespoons butter
1/4 cup olive oil
Kosher salt and freshly ground pepper
to taste
4 tablespoons minced chives

Bring salted water to a boil in a large pot. Add potatoes and garlic and bring back to a boil. Reduce heat to medium and simmer until potatoes are very tender. Drain well. Return potatoes and garlic to the pot and add sour cream, butter, olive oil, salt and pepper and mash until smooth. Garnish with chives. Serves 6.

Yellow and Green Zucchini with Sweet Red Pepper and Thyme

3 tablespoons olive oil
2 yellow zucchini, julienned
2 green zucchini, julienned
1 red bell pepper, julienned
1 sprig fresh thyme

Heat olive oil in a sauté pan over medium heat. Add remaining ingredients and sauté until tender. Serves 6.

Fresh Oregon Blackberry and Apple Cobbler

2 cups fresh blackberries
2 Gravenstein apples; peeled, cored
  and sliced
3/4 cup sugar
1/2 cup Golden Valley Pinot Noir
1 tablespoon cornstarch

Preheat oven to 425 degrees. Butter a 9-inch by 13-inch baking dish.

Combine blackberries, apples, sugar, Golden Valley Pinot Noir and cornstarch in prepared baking dish and toss together.

For the Crust:

1 cup flour
2 tablespoons sugar
1 tablespoon baking powder
1/2 teaspoon salt
6 tablespoons butter
1/2 cup buttermilk

Fresh cream

Sift together flour, sugar, baking powder and salt in a large bowl. Cut in butter until mixture resembles coarse meal. Gently fold in buttermilk, taking care not to overmix. Drop batter by spoonfuls evenly over fruit. Bake for 40 minutes or until fruit is bubbling and crust is brown. Allow to cool slightly and serve with cream. Serves 6.

GOLDEN VALLEY
BREWERY & PUB

McMINNVILLE, OREGON

One should write not unskillfully
in the running hand, be able to
sing in a pleasing voice and keep
good time to music; and lastly, a
man should not refuse a little wine
when it is pressed upon him.

YOSHIDA KENKO

Menu

"Crush" Supper

Knudsen Erath
Dry Gewürztraminer
Steamed Mussels

———

Knudsen Erath Dry Riesling
**Winter
Squash Soup**

———

Knudsen Erath Pinot Gris
**Poached Salmon
with Ginger Gris Sauce**

**Red Potatoes
Roasted
with Garlic and Sea Salt**

**Salad of Mixed
Seasonal Greens with
Raspberry Vinaigrette**

———

**Pumpkin
Ice Cream**

Knudsen Erath Winery

You would have to look hard to find a more self-effacing wine "giant" than Dick Erath, Knudsen Erath's owner and winemaker. One of the founders of Oregon's wine industry, Dick is quick to play down his role in the industry.

"The Northwest was my home as a teenager," says Dick, "and I saw how well many different types of fruit grew in this climate. It seemed to me that vinifera grapes should thrive in this environment since it so closely resembles Northern France."

Dick Erath had his first career as an electrical engineer with Tektronix Corporation and started his winemaking career by making Bordeaux-style wines in the basement of his California home. In the fall of 1967, Dick came to Oregon to purchase some Pinot Noir grapes, and the rest, as they say, is history. The quality of the wine produced so impressed Dick that he and his family purchased land almost immediately in the Dundee Hills in the northern part of Oregon's Willamette Valley. The family moved to Oregon early in 1968 and began planting their vineyard that spring.

Dick Erath and his former partner, Cal Knudsen, started Knudsen Erath Winery in 1975. At the time, there were only a few other wineries in the state. The first crush at Knudsen Erath produced a total of 216 cases of wine and three varieties; Pinot Noir, Gewürztraminer and White Riesling.

While living with his family in an unheated logger's cabin, Dick proceeded to build the original winery and the family home. Once the first cedar log structure was completed, wines were fermented and cellared in the garage, while the Erath family lived upstairs. In subsequent years, the winery has expanded to include five other buildings devoted to winemaking, case storage and aging.

From nursery propagation to bottling, Dick Erath is fully involved in the winemaking process. Dick devotes a great deal of his time to the viticultural aspects of the business, since he believes, as he says, "Great wines are made in the vineyard." After more than twenty Oregon vintages, Dick can almost taste when the time is right.

From these beginnings, the winery has become known for its quality and value—a tradition now for more than twenty years.

Steamed Mussels

1/4 pound butter
2 tablespoons garlic, minced
2 medium carrots, minced
2 celery stalks, minced
48 mussels
1/2 cup water
1/2 cup Knudsen Erath Dry
    Gewürztraminer

In a large stock pot, melt butter over medium heat. Add garlic and sauté just until fragrant. Add carrots and celery and sauté until tender. Add mussels, water, and Knudsen Erath Dry Gewürztraminer. Cover tightly and raise heat to medium high. Boil until mussels open. Discard any unopened mussels. Serve in small bowls accompanied by crusty bread. Enjoy! Serves 6.

Winter Squash Soup

2 yellow fleshed winter squash
2 cups chicken broth
1 cup Knudsen Erath Dry Riesling
1 cup plain, non-fat yogurt
Freshly ground nutmeg to taste
Salt to taste
Slices of red bell pepper for garnish
Fresh cilantro for garnish

Preheat oven to 350 degrees.

Pierce skin of squash, then bake it until tender. Peel and remove seeds. Cut into chunks and place in the bowl of a food processor or blender. Add chicken broth and Knudsen Erath Dry Riesling and process until smooth. Pour into a medium sauce pan and simmer over medium low heat for about 10 minutes or until heated through, stirring occasionally. Remove from heat and stir in yogurt, nutmeg and salt. Pour into heated bowls and garnish with a slice of red bell pepper and a sprig of cilantro. Serve with crusty bread and butter. Serves 6.

Poached Salmon with Ginger Gris Sauce

For the Salmon:

2-1/2 pounds Pacific salmon filet
1/4 cup Knudsen Erath Chardonnay
1/2 teaspoon salt

Put 3-inches of water in a roasting pan large enough to hold the salmon filet. Add the Knudsen Erath Chardonnay and salt. Bring liquid to a boil on top of the stove; add salmon, and cover with foil. Reduce heat to medium and simmer salmon until fish flakes easily, about 8 minutes per 1/2-inch thickness. Remove salmon and let cool. Slice into 6 servings.

For the Ginger Gris Sauce:

2 cups chicken stock
2 cups Knudsen Erath Pinot Gris
10 to 12 thin slices fresh ginger
3 tablespoons butter, at room
    temperature
3 tablespoons flour
2 cups heavy cream

Combine chicken stock and Knudsen Erath Pinot Gris in a medium sauce pan. Simmer over medium-high heat until reduced by half. Add the ginger, reduce heat to medium-low, and simmer for about 10 to 12 minutes. Taste to check the intensity of the ginger flavor. Remove ginger and discard.

Combine butter and flour together with a fork until smooth. Whisk into simmering stock mixture. Whisk in cream and simmer, whisking constantly until slightly thickened, do not let boil. Sauce the cooled salmon.

Red Potatoes Roasted with Garlic and Sea Salt

2 pounds small red potatoes
Olive oil
Sea salt OR coarse salt
8 cloves garlic, bruised

Preheat oven to 400 degrees.

Scrub potatoes well and leave skin on. Place in roasting pan large enough to hold potatoes in one layer. Coat with olive oil, sprinkle with salt and scatter garlic over potatoes. Roast for about 30 minutes or until tender when pierced with a skewer. Serves 6.

Salad of Mixed Seasonal Greens with Raspberry Vinaigrette

Arugula
Butter lettuce
Radicchio
Cilantro
1/4 cup roasted chopped hazelnuts
Brightly colored edible flowers such as
*   nasturtiums or pansies*

For the Raspberry Vinaigrette:

1/2 cup extra virgin olive oil
2 tablespoons raspberry vinegar
Salt and white pepper to taste

Wash and dry arugula, butter lettuce, radicchio and cilantro. Tear into bite sized pieces. Whisk together Raspberry Vinaigrette ingredients and toss with salad. Garnish with hazelnuts and edible flowers. Serves 6.

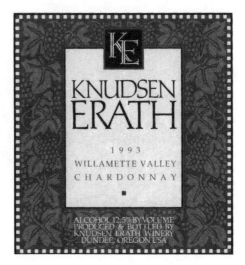

Pumpkin Ice Cream

2 eggs
1/2 cup sugar
2 cups cooked and mashed pumpkin
2 cups heavy cream
1 cup 2% milk
1/2 cup sugar
1 teaspoon vanilla extract
1/2 cup chopped toasted hazelnuts

Beat eggs with 1/2 cup sugar until pale and thick. Add pumpkin, cream, milk, 1/2 cup sugar and vanilla and beat until frothy. Pour into ice cream maker and follow manufacturer's directions. When ice cream is almost done, add hazelnuts and continue following manufacturer's directions until done. Serves 6.

Menu

FOURTH OF JULY
PICNIC

Kramer Vineyards Müller-Thurgau
Fresh fruit

———

Kramer Vineyards
Gewürztraminer
Kramer Vineyards Pinot Noir
Kramer Vineyards Chardonnay
Sausages
with Condiments

Marinated Potato Salad

Baked Beans,
purchased

Tossed Salad

———

Kramer Vineyards Raspberry Wine
Chocolate Cheesecake,
purchased

Kramer Vineyards

Located in northern Yamhill County, Kramer Vineyards is nestled in the foothills of the Coast Range. The grapes were planted starting in 1984 with initial plantings of Chardonnay, Pinot Noir, and Riesling. Subsequent plantings include Gewürztraminer, Müller-Thurgau, and Pinot Gris to total twelve acres. Caneberries are a major crop in the region. Raspberry, Blackberry, and Boysenberry wine is also produced.

Keith and Trudy Kramer are a husband and wife team who established the vineyard themselves doing the work by hand. They were serious amateur winemakers starting with berry wines and "graduating" to winegrapes in the early 1980's. Friends and family kept wanting to buy the wines by the case which led them to look for property in the wine country of Yamhill County. Keith is a pharmacist by trade and Trudy has a math/science background. After numerous amateur ribbons, they "went commercial" in 1989 producing two grape and two berry wines. The list has expanded ever since to a nice balance of sweet and dry wines.

Minimal handling with simple equipment allow us to truly hand craft our wines. Softness, yet good acid structure is a true balancing act and allows maximum fruit expression. Sometimes a little residual sugar is needed; sometimes a wine can be bone-dry. The berry wines are made in a fresh fruit style rather than a syrupy-sweet style.

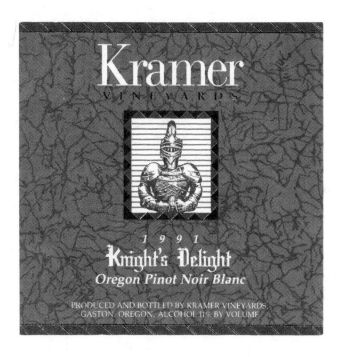

45

Picnics should have simple preparation. So many of these items can be purchased which will be easier for the chef. Picnics might appeal to more people if they only have to prepare a few things and away they go! Spending all day in the kitchen is not as much fun as being out and enjoying the day and the food.

Fresh Fruit

Combine your favorite sliced fruits such as melons, pineapple and grapes and chill.

Sausages with Condiments

Sausages such as Rabbit with garlic, Verboort or other beef sausage, Venison, or Buffalo
Large buns (regular hot dog buns are too small)
Sauerkraut
Mustard
Ketchup
Sweet relish
Sliced pickles

If sausage is uncooked then parboil for about 5 to 7 minutes to precook. Pat dry and place on a hot grill and turn every few minutes until nicely roasted. Serve with buns and lots of condiments. Napkins a must!

Who does not love wine, women, and song,
Remains a fool his whole life long.

Voss

Marinated Potato Salad

6 pounds red or white new potatoes
1/2 cup olive oil
2 tablespoons white wine vinegar
1 6-ounce jar marinated artichoke
  hearts, chopped
1/2 cup sliced black olives
1 large dill pickle, finely chopped
1 tablespoon minced fresh parsley
1 teaspoon dill
Mayonnaise

Boil potatoes in salted water until tender. Drain and peel if desired. Cut potatoes into 1-inch cubes and place in a large bowl. Combine olive oil and vinegar and pour over hot potatoes, tossing well to coat evenly. Refrigerate until cool. Add artichoke hearts, olives, pickle, parsley and dill and toss well. Add just enough mayonnaise to coat well. Refrigerate overnight to allow flavors to marry.

Tossed Salad

Several varieties of greens; washed,
  dried and torn into bite-sized
  pieces
Tomato wedges
Carrot slices
Edible flowers

1/2 cup olive oil
2 tablespoons Balsamic vinegar
1/2 teaspoon granulated garlic
Pepper to taste

Place greens, tomatoes, carrots and edible flowers in a large salad bowl. Whisk together olive oil, vinegar, garlic and pepper. Pour over salad and toss well.

Menu

The Bacchus Wine Bar's Valentine Dinner for Two

Lange Winery Pinot Gris
Mussels with Garlic Butter

———

Lange Winery Pinot Noir
Duck with Sautéed Apples

———

Crème Caramel

Lange Winery

In 1987, Don and Wendy Lange followed their hearts and palates to the north Willamette Valley of Oregon. Fueled by a passion for Pinot Noir and a love for the land, they founded their winery on 30 acres in the Red Hills above Dundee.

Their first vintage consisted of the three varietals they embrace today: Pinot Noir, Pinot Gris and Chardonnay. Lange Winery is among the first commercial producers of Pinot Gris and pioneered a barrel fermented version of the popular varietal with their first vintage back in 1987. This reserve bottling has a loyal following and Lange Winery remains the first and only producer to offer two styles of Pinot Noir.

Yamhill County, where Lange Winery is located, is home to most of Oregon's vineyards and wineries. It's no coincidence that many of the best examples of Pinot Noir in the world come from this area. The Langes planted their six acres of Pinot Noir in 1988 and 1989. It is now fully mature and producing some of the finest grapes the winery uses.

In order to supplement the fruit requirements of the winery, winemaker Don Lange works diligently with area growers to produce the best fruit under mutually agreeable conditions. This requires endless hours of walking vineyards, sampling grapes and talking to growers. He listens to their theories and concerns and shares a few of his own ideas. Often these discussions occur in the vineyard, or over a freshly prepared meal with a bottle of wine. On rare and delightful occasions, a meeting might commence stream-side, fly rod in hand, with a similarly afflicted colleague. This is how fine wine is made in the Pacific Northwest.

One of Lange Winery's grape growers also happens to be their in-state marketing representative. Wally Stein joined the operation in late 1993 bringing a wealth of marketing experience. He handles both retail and on premise sales and is an enthusiastic and helpful resource to local merchants and restaurateurs.

General manager, Wendy Lange, handles day to day office operations and facilitates all out-of-state marketing. She works closely with Wally overseeing major accounts in Oregon and can often be found, pre-dawn, on a loading dock somewhere in the Portland Metropolitan area. Between gardening and maintaining an impressive herd of dogs, she manages the tasting room and its cheerful and gracious staff.

At Lange Winery we strive to bring you the best of the north Willamette Valley. Our finely crafted wines come from vineyards planted in soils and microclimates suitable to the unique requirements of Pinot Noir, Pinot Gris and Chardonnay. The even hand of winemaker Don Lange ensures beautifully balanced wines vintage after vintage.

Established in 1982 by Joseph Balough, The Bacchus Wine Bar is the only true wine bar in the city of Portland, Oregon. Serving two dozen wines by the glass, located in the heart of Portland's historic Old Town, The Bacchus Wine Bar is an intimate dining room which brings you back to the bistros of France.

Mussels with Garlic Butter

Garlic Butter:

1/2 pound butter, at room
    temperature
1/4 pound margarine, at room
    temperature
1/4 cup minced parsley
5 cloves garlic, minced
1 tablespoon grated onion
Salt and pepper to taste

In a large bowl, combine butter, margarine, parsley, garlic, onion and salt and pepper and blend well.

For the Mussels:

1 pound mussels
2 cups Lange Winery Pinot Gris

Preheat oven to 425 degrees.

Scrub and debeard mussels. Place in a large pot. Add Lange Winery Pinot Gris, cover tightly, and bring to a boil. Shake pot a couple of times. Remove mussels as soon as they open. Discard any unopened mussels.

Place mussels in an oven-proof dish and put 1/2 teaspoon garlic butter on each mussel. Place in the oven until butter starts to bubble. Serve immediately with French bread as an accompaniment. Serves 2.

Duck with Sautéed Apples

1 3-1/2-pound duck
1 tablespoon butter
4 large mushrooms, sliced
2/3 cup heavy cream
1/4 cup blackberry wine
1/4 cup Lange Winery Pinot Noir
1 ounce Montrachet
    OR other goat cheese
1/8 teaspoon cayenne
Salt and pepper to taste
Chopped walnuts

Preheat oven to 325 degrees.

Remove the giblets and neck skin from duck and save for another use. Cut duck in half lengthwise. Place in a pot of cold water. Bring to a boil over high heat, then reduce heat to medium-high and simmer for 15 minutes. Drain well and discard liquid. Remove skin and discard. Place duck in a roasting pan and roast until done, about 15 minutes.

Melt butter in a skillet over medium heat. Add mushrooms and sauté until tender. Add cream and reduce by half. Add blackberry wine and Lange Winery Pinot Noir and reduce by half. Whisk in Montrachet until smooth. Add cayenne, salt and pepper.

Divide the sauce between two plates. Place half a duck on sauce and sprinkle with chopped walnuts. Serves 2.

The wine urges me on, the bewitching wine,
which sets even a wise man to singing and
to laughing gently and rouses him up to dance
and brings forth words which were better left
unspoken.

HOMER

Sautéed Apples

1 Granny Smith apple, peeled,
    cored and cut into wedges
1 tablespoon butter
1 teaspoon sugar
1/4 cup Lange Winery Pinot Noir

Melt butter in a sauté pan over medium heat. Add sugar and cook until golden. Add Lange Winery Pinot Noir, and reduce until the consistency of syrup. Add apple and simmer until the apple is very tender, turning once.

Crème Caramel

3/4 cup sugar
1 tablespoon water
1 small orange, peeled, halved
    and thinly sliced
2-1/2 cups milk
Zest of 1 small orange
3 whole eggs
1 egg yolk
1/4 cup sugar

Preheat oven to 400 degrees.

Combine 3/4 cup sugar and water in a small, heavy saucepan. Cook over high heat, swirling pan a couple of times, until sugar has caramelized and is a dark golden brown. Place half of an orange slice in the bottom of 6 custard dishes. Divide the caramel between the dishes and pour over orange slices.

Heat milk and orange zest in a medium sauce pan over medium-low heat for 10 minutes. Strain and discard orange zest.

In a medium bowl, beat the eggs, egg yolk and 1/4 cup sugar together until light. Stir in the strained milk until smooth. Fill custard cups with milk mixture. Place custard cups in a large baking pan and add hot water to come halfway up the sides of the custard dishes. Bake for 40 to 45 minutes, or until set. Cool before placing in the refrigerator. Chill thoroughly before serving. Serves 6.

Menu

FATHER'S FAVORITES FOR FATHER'S DAY

*Laurel Ridge 1988 Brut,
Méthode Champenoise*
Chicken Liver Pâte
with Currants

———

*Laurel Ridge 1991 Reserve
Sauvignon Blanc*
Citrus, Sweet Onion and
Blue Cheese Salad

———

Laurel Ridge Pinot Noir
Marinated
Flank Steak

Red Potatoes Roasted
with Garlic Butter

Steamed Carrots
with Dill

———

*Laurel Ridge Cuvée Blanc, Extra Dry,
Méthode Champenoise*
Fruit Tart

Laurel Ridge Winery

First selected in the 1880's by a German winemaking family, the site for Laurel Ridge Winery is one of the most historic and picturesque in Oregon. With a commanding view of the Tualatin Valley, the vineyard in Washington County produces wine from some of Oregon's oldest vines.

Although the original vineyard was a casualty of Prohibition, it was one of the first vineyards re-planted in the 1960's when Oregon was rediscovered as one of the world's best cool climate viticultural regions. The vineyard now produces Pinot Noir, Gewürztraminer, Riesling, Semillon, and Sylvaner grapes. Another 25 acres are being prepared for plantings of Pinot Noir and Chardonnay. The vineyard and historic farmhouse are under the ownership of Mr. and Mrs. Mylan Stoyanov. A sister vineyard owned by David Teppola in Yamhill County contains 50 acres of Sauvignon Blanc, Riesling and Pinot Noir. Between the two vineyards, the winery is able to control the growing of almost all its grapes.

Laurel Ridge Winery was started in 1986 as a partnership between three families. Over time, the ownership of the winery company has been consolidated in Mr. and Mrs. David Teppola. David Teppola presides over the winery on a daily basis and acts as the general manager, overseeing both the vineyard and the winery operations.

For the last four years, Laurel Ridge wines have been made by Paul Gates, an enologist who graduated from Fresno State University. The winery produces several premium varietal wines, but is equally well known for its two Méthode Champenoise, sparkling wines. Cuvée Blanc, an off-dry sparkling Riesling, is the perfect wine for receptions, banquets, toasts, and casual entertaining. Brut, the more elegant, and formal sparkler is 90% Pinot Noir and 10% Pinot Blanc. All wines are available for tasting in the tasting room in the winery.

The original farmhouse, built in three stages starting in 1883, is currently undergoing a complete restoration. Upon completion it will contain the tasting room, banquet facilities, winery offices, and a private apartment.

Chicken Liver Pâte with Currants

1/3 cup currants
3 tablespoons Cognac
3 tablespoons Port
2 tablespoons butter
1 pound fresh chicken livers, trimmed
1 clove garlic
1 teaspoon salt
1/4 teaspoon white pepper
1/2 teaspoon fresh thyme
6 tablespoons butter, at room
    temperature
Melted butter

Soak the currants in the Cognac and Port overnight. Drain and reserve liquid and currants in separate bowls.

Melt 2 tablespoons butter in a large sauté pan over medium heat. Add chicken livers and sauté until nicely browned but still pink inside. Remove chicken livers with a slotted spoon and allow to cool. Add garlic to pan and sauté just until fragrant. Pour in reserved Cognac and Port and deglaze pan. Whisk in salt, pepper and thyme and bring to a simmer. Simmer for 1 minute then pour over livers. Let cool completely.

Place in the bowl of a food processor and process until smooth. Do not overprocess. Add currants and 6 tablespoons butter and pulse just until well mixed. Pack pâte into a serving bowl or crock and pour a little melted butter over the top to seal. Chill for at least 24 hours before serving. Serve with French bread.

Citrus, Sweet Onion and Bleu Cheese Salad

6 to 8 cups mixed greens torn into
    bite-sized pieces (no Iceburg lettuce
    please)
2 oranges; peeled, sectioned and all
    white pith removed
2 Mandarin oranges; peeled, sectioned
    and all white pith removed
2 grapefruit; peeled, sectioned and all
    white pith removed
2 sweet red onions OR Walla Walla
    sweet onions, thinly sliced
8 ounces bleu cheese, crumbled
Italian salad dressing

For each serving place about 1 cup greens on a salad plate. Top with 3 to 5 slices mixed citrus fruit. Place 3 or 4 slices onion on top. Sprinkle 1 ounce bleu cheese on top. Immediately before serving drizzle with Italian dressing. Serves 8.

Marinated Flank Steak

2 large flank steaks, lightly scored on
   both sides
2 cups Laurel Ridge Pinot Noir
2 tablespoons Worcestershire sauce
3 tablespoons molasses
2 teaspoons salt OR 1/4 cup light soy
   sauce

Combine Laurel Ridge Pinot Noir, Worcestershire sauce, molasses and salt and whisk until smooth. Divide marinade between two shallow glass or other non-reactive dishes. Place a flank steak in each dish and cover with plastic wrap. Refrigerate at least 12 hours or overnight, turning several times.

Remove steaks from marinade and discard marinade. Broil or barbecue steaks about 5 minutes on each side (depending on thickness). Steak will be medium-rare. Slice meat across the grain at an angle so that the slices look thicker than the steak was. Place sliced steak on a heated serving platter and pour any meat juices over the top. Serves 8.

Red Potatoes Roasted with Garlic Butter

16 medium red potatoes, scrubbed
8 tablespoons butter
4 cloves garlic, minced
Salt and pepper to taste

Preheat oven to 325 degrees. Lightly oil two 9-inch by 13-inch glass or other non-reactive baking dishes with olive oil.

Arrange potatoes in dishes so they do not touch. Melt butter and garlic together in a small sauce pan. Drizzle over potatoes. Season with salt and pepper. Roast for 60 to 75 minutes, or until tines of a meat fork pierces easily to center of potato. Turn potatoes once or twice during roasting. Serves 8.

Steamed Carrots with Dill

8 medium carrots, peeled and sliced
2 tablespoons butter
1/2 teaspoon dill
Salt to taste

Steam carrots until tender but firm. Remove to a heated serving bowl and toss with butter, dill and salt. Serves 8.

Fruit Tart

For the Pastry:

1-1/3 cups flour
1/2 cup sugar
1 teaspoon lemon zest, finely minced
1/2 cup cold butter
1 egg yolk

Preheat oven to 300 degrees.

In a large bowl, stir together flour, sugar, and 1 teaspoon lemon zest. Cut in butter until mixture resembles coarse meal. Stir in egg yolk until dough forms a ball. Press dough into 11-inch tart pan with a removable bottom or a 10-inch spring-form pan. Bake for 30 minutes or until golden brown. Let cool completely.

For the Filling:

3 ounces cream cheese, softened
1 cup heavy cream
1/4 cup powdered sugar
1/2 teaspoon lemon zest, finely minced
1 teaspoon fresh lemon juice
1/4 teaspoon vanilla extract
1/4 teaspoon almond extract
3 to 4 cups fresh fruit in season such as strawberries, blueberries or raspberries or a combination. Canned peaches or pears also work well.
2/3 cup currant OR apple jelly
Slivered almonds or hazelnuts

In a large bowl combine cream cheese and cream and blend slowly until smooth. Add powdered sugar, 1/2 teaspoon lemon zest, lemon juice, vanilla extract and almond extract and beat until stiff. Spread mixture in cooled tart crust.

Arrange fruit artfully on top of cream cheese mixture. Melt currant jelly over low heat and cool slightly. Drizzle jelly over fruit. Sprinkle with almonds. Remove tart from pan and serve. Serves 8.

Which food with which wine? Matching wine with food depends a lot on how the food is seasoned; is it spicy, is it sweet? White with fish and red with beef is not the golden rule. Most important though, is for you to drink what you like and what tastes good with the foods you like! We have made some suggestions for enjoying Laurel Ridge wines. Experiment and have fun!

Cuvée Blanc:
Oysters, Chicken, Goat Cheese and Bread,
Crab Stuffed Pastry Puffs, Fresh Fruit Desserts

Brut:
Oysters, Prawns, Swordfish,
Winter Squash Soup, Fruit Tarts, Cheese Fondue

Sauvignon Blanc:
Salmon, Pork, Chicken, Fettucine with Creamy Sauces,
Wild Mushrooms, Green Salad with Pine Nuts and Feta Cheese

Pinot Blanc:
Grilled Prawns, Fresh Tuna,
Potato Leek Soup, Fettucine with Light Cream Sauce

Chardonnay:
Salmon, Shellfish,
Dofino Cheese, Light Creamy Pastas

Gewürztraminer:
Pork, Sausage, Oriental Cuisine,
Cajun Dishes, Melon with Jalapeño Sorbet

Riesling:
Goat Cheese, Mild Cheeses with Bread,
Wonton Soup, Melon with Proscuitto, Green Salad with Apples and Nuts

Pinot Noir:
Pork, Veal, Lamb, Duck, Rabbit,
Fettucine with Asparagus and Shiitaki Mushrooms,
Ravioli Stuffed with Cheese and Spinach, Chocolate!!!

Menu

EASTER BRUNCH

Madrona View Blanc De Noir
Madrona View Chardonnay
Citrus Fruit
Terrine

Prosciutto
Breakfast Strata

Spinach and
Mushroom Crêpes
with Gruyère Cream Sauce

Chicken with
Port and Shallots

———

Madrona View
Columbia Valley Cabernet
Chocolate Truffle Cake
with
Hazelnut Crème Anglaise

Madrona Hill Vineyards and Winery

Madrona Hill Vineyards and Winery is located in Portland, Oregon. We have temporarily moved to a building in the center of town, but will eventually build next to our vineyards in Amity Hills above Amity, Oregon. Madrona Hill Vineyards has an acre of Cabernet grapes planted in 1976 with 3 acres of Pinot Noir grapes planted more recently. We also lease 15 acres of Riesling, Pinot Noir and Chardonnay in Eola Hills. Grapes are also purchased from other choice vineyards throughout Oregon and Southeast Washington. We make wine from the best grapes grown in these regions. In 1992, we topped our production with 5,000 cases of wine, which is small even for Oregon. Even though we take our wine making seriously, we enjoy having fun exploring the world of wine making. This helps diversify our line of wines, from a Port to a Sparkling Muscat.

Unlike other Oregon wineries, we have specialized in the Muscat grape. From Eastern Washington we buy the Muscat Caneli to make our Muscat and Pearl of Muscat, a fortified wine. Our Oregon Spumante is made from the "early Muscat" grape of the Willamette Valley. Also from Eastern Washington, we receive some of our Cabernet Sauvignon grapes. The sandy soil and a sunny climate with cool evenings is a good combination for a rich and silky Cabernet. Some micro-climates in Oregon can also produce great Cabernet with interesting flavors. Cabernet is the basic grape used in our Port. It is made in small oak barrels using some of the same traditional methods as in Portugal to make a strong, deep purple wine.

Sometimes we stumble on a good find as with our 1992 Late Harvest Gewürztraminer. The grapes were harvested at super-ripeness with a coating of Botrytis (Noble Rot) to make a sweet, luscious dessert wine.

The owners, William (Mikey) Jones and Micheal Straus work full time at the winery. Mikey is the winemaker and oversees the vineyards. Micheal's main responsibility is outside sales, traveling the state and making a pitch to store owners and restaurants. Both men wear many different hats at the winery and share the responsibility of getting the job done. Our motto is: "At Madrona Hill we believe it does not take a lot of capital to make good wine, just good luck and good friends."

Citrus Fruit Terrine

4 oranges
2 ruby grapefruit
Zest of 1 orange, julienned
1 cup sugar
2/3 cup water
1-1/2 cups Madrona View Oregon
  Spumante
2 tablespoons unflavored gelatin
1/3 cup cold water

Prepare the oranges and grapefruit by removing the rind and all of the white pith that surrounds the fruit. Separate the fruit sections and cut away the membrane between each section. Put orange and grapefruit sections in separate bowls.

Place the orange zest in a small saucepan and cover with water. Bring to a boil and boil for 3 minutes. Drain and reserve the blanched zest, discard the blanching liquid.

Combine the sugar and 2/3 cup water in the small sauce pan. Bring to a boil. Reduce heat to medium and simmer for 2 minutes. Add reserved orange zest and simmer 5 minutes.

Dissolve gelatin in 1/3 cup cold water and let stand 5 minutes to soften gelatin. Remove syrup from heat and stir in softened gelatin. Stir in Madrona View Oregon Spumante. Allow foam to subside and cool completely. This mixture will be the aspic.

Pour a little of the aspic in the bottom of a terrine mold or a bread pan. Chill until set. Dip the orange sections in the aspic and put one layer on top of the aspic layer. Chill until almost set. Repeat with one layer of grapefruit. Repeat until all fruit and aspic is used, always waiting until each layer sets before adding the next. Chill overnight before serving.

To serve, dip mold in hot water turn out onto a platter. Slice about 3/4-inch thick and serve. Serves 8.

Prosciutto Breakfast Strata

12 ounces Oregon blue cheese,
  crumbled
12 ounces cream cheese, softened and
  cut into small pieces
2-1/2 cups milk
5 eggs
2 teaspoons dried rosemary, crumbled
1/2 teaspoon white pepper
1/4 teaspoon Tabasco sauce
1 tablespoon olive oil
10 ounces Prosciutto, chopped
1 16-ounce loaf challah bread, cut into
  2-inch cubes and toasted

Preheat oven to 350 degrees. Lightly butter a 2-quart baking dish.

In a large bowl, combine blue cheese, cream cheese, milk, eggs, 1-1/2 teaspoons rosemary, white pepper and Tabasco sauce and beat on low speed until mixture is somewhat smooth. Heat olive oil in a small sauté pan, add Prosciutto and sauté lightly. Stir all but 2 tablespoons of the Prosciutto into the egg mixture. Place the toasted challah into the prepared baking dish and pour egg mixture over. Allow to stand for 30 minutes. Sprinkle with remaining rosemary and Prosciutto. Bake for about 40 minutes or until custard is set. Serves 8.

Spinach and Mushroom Crêpes with Gruyère Cream Sauce

For the Crêpes:

3/4 cup flour
1/8 teaspoon salt
2 eggs
2 tablespoons melted butter
1 cup milk
Butter for cooking the crêpes

Sift the flour and salt into a large bowl and make a well in the center. Place eggs, melted butter and 1/2 cup milk in the well. Starting from the center, whisk ingredients together until smooth. Pour in remaining 1/2 cup milk and whisk vigorously until batter is smooth. Cover and refrigerate at least 1 hour or overnight before cooking the crêpes.

Heat an 8-inch crêpe pan over medium-high heat. Lightly brush with melted butter. Pour in about 3 tablespoons batter and tilt the pan in all directions to coat the bottom evenly. Cook until the top looks dry and brown spots appear on the bottom, about 2 minutes. Turn with a spatula and cook until top has set, about 1 minute. Remove crêpe to a plate and cover with a towel to keep warm. Repeat with remaining batter and stack finished crêpes on plate.

For the Filling:

4 tablespoons butter
1/4 cup minced onion
1-1/2 pounds mushrooms, sliced or
    quartered if small
1 10-ounce package frozen chopped
    spinach, thawed and squeezed dry
2 tablespoons fresh lemon juice
1/4 teaspoon freshly grated nutmeg
1 teaspoon salt
1/4 teaspoon white pepper
1/2 cup heavy cream

Melt the butter in a large skillet over medium heat. Add the onion and sauté until translucent. Add mushrooms and sauté until mushrooms give off their liquid and continue cooking until most of the liquid has evaporated. Add spinach, lemon juice, nutmeg, salt and white pepper and sauté until most of the liquid has evaporated. Stir in cream and simmer until most of the liquid has evaporated. Cool mixture before filling the crêpes.

For the Gruyère Cream Sauce:

1 tablespoon butter
1 tablespoon flour
1 cup milk
1/4 cup cream
1-1/2 cups shredded Gruyère cheese
Paprika

Melt the butter in a medium sauce pan over medium heat. Whisk in the flour and cook until bubbly. Add the milk gradually, whisking constantly. Whisk in the cream. Cook, whisking constantly until mixture thickens. Remove from heat and stir in the Gruyère until smooth.

To Assemble the Crêpes:

Preheat oven to 350 degrees. Lightly butter a 9-inch by 13-inch baking dish.

Place about 3 tablespoons filling in each crêpe and roll up. Place rolled crêpe, seam side down, in prepared baking dish. Continue until all crêpes and filling are used. Pour sauce over and sprinkle lightly with paprika. Bake for about 20 to 30 minutes or until hot and bubbly. Serves 8.

> **A meal without wine is like a day without sunshine.**
> BRILLAT-SAVARIN

Chicken with Port and Shallots

4 tablespoons butter
8 boneless chicken breasts
Salt and pepper
4 shallots, minced
2 cups Madrona View Oregon Vin
　　Doux Natural Cabernet
　　Sauvignon "Port Style"

Heat butter in a large skillet over medium heat. Season chicken breasts with salt and pepper. Sauté chicken until golden brown on both sides. Remove to a platter and keep warm. Add shallots to pan and sauté until translucent. Pour in Madrona View Oregon Vin Doux Natural and deglaze pan, whisking up any browned bits. Return chicken to pan and simmer for about 20 minutes or until done. Remove to a serving platter and keep warm. Reduce sauce by one half and pour over chicken. Serves 8.

Chocolate Truffle Cake

1-2/3 cups semi-sweet chocolate chips
9 tablespoons butter
8 egg yolks
3/4 cup sugar
8 egg whites
Pinch salt
1/4 cup sugar
5 tablespoons flour, sifted

Preheat oven to 350 degrees. Generously butter an 11-inch spring-form pan and line the bottom with parchment paper and butter the parchment.

Melt the chocolate and butter together in the top of a double-boiler over medium-low heat. Whisk until smooth and allow to cool.

In a medium bowl, beat the egg yolks and 3/4 cup sugar together until very light and thick. Stir in the cooled chocolate mixture until smooth.

In a large bowl, beat the egg whites with the pinch of salt until stiff but not dry. Gradually add the 1/4 cup sugar and continue beating until sugar dissolves.

Sprinkle flour over beaten egg whites. Pour chocolate mixture over egg whites. Carefully fold together just until combined, taking care not to deflate egg whites. Pour batter into prepared springform pan. Bake for about 40 minutes or until top is cracked and cake begins to pull away from the sides. Let cool in pan before unmolding.

Place about 1/4 cup Hazelnut Crème Anglaise (see page 63) on a dessert plate and top with a slice of Chocolate Truffle Cake. Sprinkle with powdered sugar and serve. Serves 10.

Hazelnut Crème Anglaise

2 cups milk
3/4 cup sugar
1/2 cup sliced hazelnuts, lightly toasted
1 teaspoon vanilla extract
6 egg yolks

Combine milk, sugar, hazelnuts and vanilla in a medium sauce pan. Bring to a simmer over medium heat, whisking to dissolve the sugar. Place egg yolks in a bowl and whisk lightly. When milk mixture comes to a gentle boil, ladle about 1/2 cup of the mixture into the egg yolks and whisk until smooth. Pour egg yolk mixture back into the sauce pan. Reduce heat to medium-low and stir with a wooden spoon until mixture thickens and coats the back of the spoon. Take care not to overcook mixture. Remove from heat and pour into a bowl that is sitting inside a larger bowl of ice. Stir gently until cool. Chill before serving. Makes about 3 cups.

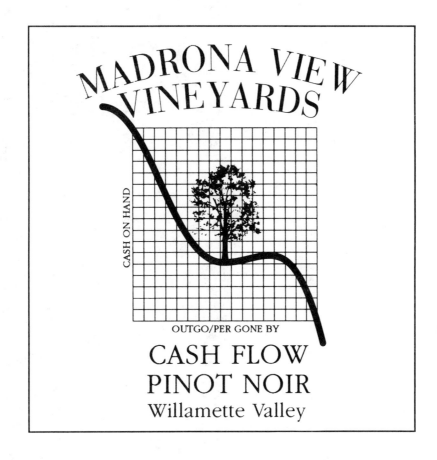

Menu

SUMMER BARBECUE IN THE VINEYARD

McKinlay Vineyards Chardonnay
Grape Leaves Stuffed
with Shrimp

Easy
Stuffed Mushrooms

McKinlay Vineyards Pinot Noir
Tossed
Green Salad

Rolled Chicken
with Sorrel and Spinach

Oven Roasted
Potatoes

Corn on the Cob

Gingerbread with
Whipped Cream and Berries

McKinlay Vineyards

OREGON

PINOT NOIR

WILLAMETTE VALLEY

ALCOHOL 12.5% BY VOLUME

Grape Leaves Stuffed with Shrimp

For the Marinade:

1/2 cup McKinlay Vineyards
    Chardonnay
2 tablespoons dark sesame oil
3 cloves garlic, minced
1 tablespoon minced fresh ginger
1/2 teaspoon salt
1/8 teaspoon pepper
32 medium shrimp, peeled and
    deveined
16 large grape leaves

Whisk together marinade ingredients until smooth. Add shrimp and marinate at least 3 hours or overnight.

Wash and trim stems from grape leaves. Soak in cold water for 15 minutes. Drain and pat dry with paper towels. Wrap 2 shrimp in each grape leaf along with a little of the marinade. Tie with string. Grill for 10 to 15 minutes, turning to cook on all sides. Serves 8.

Easy Stuffed Mushrooms

24 medium Crimini mushrooms
    OR white mushrooms
1/2 cup Gorgonzola cheese
    OR other blue cheese
1 green onion (including the green
    part), sliced
Salt and pepper to taste
48 pinenuts

Wipe mushrooms clean and remove the stems. Place mushroom caps in a single layer in a baking dish, stem side up. Place mushroom stems, Gorgonzola, green onion, salt and pepper in the bowl of a food processor and process until smooth. Divide filling evenly among the mushrooms. Top with pinenuts. Broil for about 10 minutes or until hot and bubbly. Serves 8.

Chicken Roll with Sorrel and Spinach

2 whole chickens
2 cups chopped fresh spinach
2 cups chopped fresh sorrel
1/2 cup chopped fresh sage
4 green onions (including the green
    part), chopped
1 teaspoon finely grated lemon zest
Salt and pepper to taste

Have your butcher bone chickens, leaving skin intact as possible.

In a large bowl, combine spinach, sorrel, sage, green onions and lemon zest and mix well.

Lay chicken skin side down on a cutting board. Salt and pepper the meat generously. Spread one half of the spinach mixture on each chicken. Roll up tightly, tucking in any stray flaps, and tie with kitchen string to secure. Grill over indirect heat until internal temperature reaches 160 degrees, about 1 hour. Allow to stand for 10 minutes before slicing. Serves 8.

Oven Roasted Potatoes

32 small red potatoes, scrubbed well
8 to 10 cloves garlic, peeled and
*   smashed*
3 tablespoons olive oil
Salt and pepper to taste

Preheat oven to 350 degrees.

Place all ingredients in a heavy skillet or a Dutch oven with a lid. Cover and cook over medium heat, shaking pan often. Remove lid and bake in oven for 50 to 60 minutes or until very tender. Serves 8.

A true German can't stand the French,
Yet willingly he drinks their wines.

GOETHE

Gingerbread with Whipped Cream and Berries

Gingerbread goes very well with Pinot Noir. This is an excellent finish to a summer meal.

1/2 cup sugar
1/4 cup butter
1/4 cup shortening
1 egg, beaten
2-1/2 cups flour
1-1/2 teaspoons baking soda
2 teaspoons cinnamon
2 teaspoons ground ginger
1 teaspoon ground cloves
1/2 teaspoon salt
1-1/3 cups boiling water
2/3 cup molasses

Whipped Cream
Fresh strawberries or raspberries

Preheat oven to 350 degrees. Grease a 13-inch by 9-inch baking dish.

In a large bowl, cream together sugar, butter, shortening and egg until light and fluffy. In a small bowl sift together the flour, baking soda, cinnamon, ginger, cloves and salt. In a 2-cup measuring cup, stir together the boiling water and molasses.

Add the flour mixture and molasses mixture to the creamed mixture alternately, beating well after each addition. Pour into prepared baking dish. Bake for about 50 to 60 minutes, or until toothpick inserted in the center comes out clean. Top with a dollop of whipped cream and fresh berries.

Menu

BUD BREAK CELEBRATION DINNER

Montinore Vineyards Pinot Gris
Walla Walla
Sweet Onion Tart

———

Montinore Vineyards Pinot Noir
Grilled Beef Tenderloin
Marinated in
Pinot Noir, Garlic and Rosemary

Sunwarmed Pasta
with Tomatoes and Basil

———

Fabulous Brownies
with Chantilly Cream

Montinore Vineyards

The Montinore Wine Estate, started in 1982, owes its beginnings to the explosive devastation of Mount St. Helens. When the May 1980 eruption covered fields with ash and destroyed the growing crops, the owners began to consider other uses for their acreage. After an intensive study proved the potential for world-class wines from this unique property, 450,000 vines were nursery-propagated in 1983. Winemaking began in 1987 when the first fruits were produced from those young vines. A new, state-of-the-art winery facility was added in 1990, and today Montinore ranks as one of Oregon's largest producers of high-quality, handmade wines.

Great wines begin in the vineyards, where the vineyard manager, Ron Engle, puts his expertise to work to bring the finest grapes possible from each variety each year. Once the grapes leave the vine, it is the knowledge, dedication and skill of the winemaker that turn great grapes into great wines. At Montinore, winemaking is entrusted to Jacques Tardy, who trained in viticulture and enology at Lycée Agricole, Beaune, France. Drawn to Oregon by its growing reputation for Pinot Noir, Tardy joined Montinore in 1990 "to create a Pinot Noir of international acclaim." Tardy blends European craftsmanship and tradition with innovation and state-of-the-art techniques and equipment in creating Montinore's award winning wines.

Pinot Noir, Chardonnay and Pinot Gris are the most prominent varieties grown at Montinore, but it also produces award-winning wines with its estate-grown White Riesling, Müller-Thurgau, Gewürztraminer and Chenin Blanc.

From grape-growing to winemaking, Montinore's emphasis is on creating wines with styles and structures that combine with a wide variety of cuisines. Its innovative techniques and dedication to quality have placed Montinore Vineyards at the forefront of American wineries in the quest to produce world-class wines.

Walla Walla Sweet Onion Tart

For the Tart:

1/4 pound butter
3 medium Walla Walla sweet onions,
*   thinly sliced*
3 cups half and half OR heavy cream
4 eggs, beaten
1 teaspoon dry mustard
1/4 teaspoon Worcestershire sauce
1/8 teaspoon white pepper
Salt to taste
One 9-inch unbaked pastry shell

Preheat oven to 350 degrees.

Heat butter in a large skillet over medium-low heat. Add onions and sauté until golden brown, don't let them get too dark.

In a large bowl whisk together the half and half and eggs until smooth. Whisk in the mustard, Worcestershire sauce, white pepper and salt.

Place the cooked onions in the bottom of the pastry shell, distributing evenly. Place pastry shell on a baking sheet and place in the center of the oven. Pour in the half and half mixture, being careful not to spill over the sides. Bake for about 45 minutes, or until golden brown and center is firm to the touch. Remove from oven and cool on a rack for 15 to 25 minutes before slicing. Serve with a dollop of Red Pepper Sauce. Serves 8.

For the Red Pepper Sauce:

2 cups plain yogurt
1 red bell pepper, roasted, peeled and
*   seeded*
1 clove garlic, minced
Salt and white pepper to taste

Combine all ingredients in the bowl of a food processor and process until smooth.

Alonso of Aragon was wont to say
in commendation of age,
that age appears to be best in four things—
old wood best to burn,
old wine to drink,
old friends to trust,
and old authors best to read.

BACON

Grilled Beef Tenderloin Marinated in Pinot Noir, Garlic and Rosemary

1 whole beef tenderloin, 4 pounds,
   tail and head secured with kitchen
   twine

For the Marinade:

2 cups extra virgin olive oil
1 cup Montinore Vineyards Pinot Noir
1/2 medium red onion, sliced
3 shallots, minced
3 cloves garlic, minced
2 bay leaves, crumbled
1 tablespoon freshly cracked black
   peppercorns
2 sprigs fresh rosemary, minced
   OR 1-1/2 tablespoons dry rosemary

Place beef in a glass or ceramic dish. Whisk together the marinade ingredients and pour over meat. Cover with plastic wrap and refrigerate overnight.

Heat charcoal in a barbecue or broiler to high, with grill at least 3 inches from heat. Remove beef from marinade. Strain marinade. Pat dry with paper towels and let warm to room temperature before grilling.

Place meat on grill and cook for 30 minutes, basting with marinade, turning to sear on all sides. Do not over cook.

Remove from grill, remove twine and let stand for 10 minutes. Slice across grain and drizzle with 1 teaspoon extra virgin olive oil if desired. Serves 8.

Sunwarmed Pasta with Tomatoes and Basil

The first sunny day of spring, this recipe comes to mind. I look forward to preparing this as a sign that summer is on the way. Caution: this recipe is addictive, you'll be making it often.

5 large tomatoes, diced
15-ounce wheel of Brie cheese, torn
   into bite-sized pieces
1 cup fresh basil, sliced into strips
3 cloves garlic, minced
3/4 cup olive oil
1/2 teaspoon salt
1 teaspoon freshly ground pepper
1-1/2 pounds fettucine
1 tablespoon olive oil
1 teaspoon salt
Freshly grated Parmesan cheese

In a large bowl, combine tomatoes, Brie, basil, garlic, olive oil, 1/2 teaspoon salt and pepper. Cover and let stand at room temperature for 2 hours.

Fifteen minutes before serving, bring 6 quarts water with 1 tablespoon olive oil and 1 teaspoon salt and cook pasta until al dente. Test for doneness by tossing one strand towards the wall, if it sticks to the wall, it is fini (old Italian method).

Drain pasta and immediately toss with the tomato mixture. Serve at once sprinkled with Parmesan. Serve with crusty bread. Serves 8.

Fabulous Brownies with Chantilly Cream

For those who have discovered the chocolate and Pinot Noir addiction, this Brownie is the perfect chocolate dessert. For you that have yet to try this combination, take a bite of brownie and enjoy the rich chocolate smoothness. With the lingering chocolate flavors still on the palate, take a sip of Montinore Vineyards Winemakers Reserve Pinot Noir. You won't believe the fabulous flavor combination. I no longer think just chocolate, but chocolate and Pinot Noir.

For the Brownies:

1-1/3 cups sugar
1 cup packed light brown sugar
14-1/2 tablespoons butter
4 ounces unsweetened chocolate
1-3/4 tablespoons light corn syrup
1 cup flour
1 teaspoon baking powder
4 large eggs, at room temperature
2 teaspoons vanilla extract
Toasted and chopped hazelnuts

Preheat oven to 350 degrees. Line a 9-inch by 13-inch baking pan with foil so that the foil extends 2 inches over the sides of the pan. Lightly butter the bottom and sides of the foil.

In a medium sauce pan, combine sugar, brown sugar, butter, chocolate and corn syrup. Melt together over low heat until smooth, stirring often with a wooden spoon. Remove from heat and let cool.

When cool add the eggs, one at a time beating well after each addition. Beat in the vanilla. In another bowl, stir the flour and baking powder together with a fork. Stir into the chocolate mixture until smooth.

Pour batter into prepared pan and bake for 30 to 40 minutes or until toothpick inserted in the center comes out clean. Cool in the pan for 30 minutes. Remove the brownies from the pan by lifting the ends of foil. Cool in foil on rack for 2 hours. Invert the Brownies on a large cutting board. Gently peel off the foil. Invert again and cut into small squares.

For the Chantilly Cream:

1 cup heavy cream, chilled
3 tablespoons sugar
1 teaspoon vanilla extract

Beat heavy cream until soft peaks form. Beat in sugar and vanilla until sugar dissolves. Top each brownie square with Chantilly Cream and garnish with hazelnuts. Serves 8.

Bud break comes in early spring. In 1994 bud break came on March 30th. In a normal year the following sequence of events should occur:

1.

Bloom should come 90 days after bud break.

2.

Version (the grapes start turning and maturing) should begin 60 days after bloom.

3.

Harvest should take place 30 days after version.

We should be able to harvest starting in early September and be through by the end of October. September and October are predictably great weather for harvesting grapes in the Willamette Valley of Oregon.

RON ENGLE,
VINEYARD MANAGER

Menu

SOKOL BLOSSER WINE COUNTRY
CINCO DE MAYO

Sokol Blosser 1991
Yamhill County Pinot Noir
Pavo (Turkey)
Mole Rojo

———

Sokol Blosser 1993
Yamhill County Müller-Thurgau
Chilies Rellenos
Linda

———

Sokol Blosser 1992
Yamhill County Chardonnay
or
Sokol Blosser 1992
Yamhill County Gewürztraminer
Tequila
Lime Shrimp

———

Susan's
Mango Salsa

Sokol Blosser Winery

Susan Sokol and Bill Blosser started their vineyard in 1971 and Sokol Blosser Winery in 1977, combining their names and talents to establish what has become one of Oregon's largest and best known wineries. "There was no Oregon wine industry when we started," says Susan. Susan and Bill are among the early Oregon pioneers who helped make Oregon wine internationally famous.

Why Oregon? The hillside vineyards, with their gentle slopes, are the perfect growing area for the Burgundian and Germanic grape varieties: Pinot Noir, Chardonnay, White Riesling, Gewürztraminer, Müller-Thurgau. The grapes for Sokol Blosser wines come only from the heart of Oregon wine country: Durant Vineyards, Hyland Vineyards, and Sokol Blosser Vineyards—three of the oldest and best vineyards in Yamhill County. These three vineyards have consistently produced grapes with wonderful flavor and maturity which have, under the careful eye of winemaker John Haw, resulted in wines of elegance and distinction. Sokol Blosser wines have won gold medals at such major competitions as London's International Wine & Spirits Competition; San Francisco State Fair; Dallas *Morning News* National Competition; Atlanta International Wine Festival; and the Grand National Wine Competition.

Wine production at Sokol Blosser relies on traditional and conservative procedures assisted, rather than controlled, by technology. Grapes are hand-harvested, brought in small wooden totes to the winery, and treated as gently as possible to deliver their full flavor potential. Both Pinot Noir and Chardonnay are aged in small (60 gallon) French oak casks for up to 12 months. The limited "Redland" bottling is composed of the very best barrels and is specially selected to represent the finest of each variety.

Visitors are welcome to enjoy Sokol Blosser's popular Tasting Room. The Sokol Blosser Winery, Tasting Room, and vineyards are located just 40 minutes from Portland off Highway 99W. A short drive up the hill puts you in the heart of wine country, surrounded by vineyards, lush lawns, and shady trees, with a sweeping view of the Willamette Valley and its backdrop of snow-capped Cascade Mountains.

Sokol Blosser's Walk-Through Showcase Vineyard, the first of its kind in the Northwest, offers visitors a self-guided tour that explains the wine grape varieties and describes the different seasons of the vineyard. During the fall, visitors are able to taste ripe grapes from the Showcase Vineyard as well as sample wines made from those varieties in the Tasting Room.

Food with the "south of the border" influence abound in the Oregon wine country, and happen to be the cuisine of choice at many Sokol Blosser employee gatherings. It is said that wine is no match for this style of eating, but may we suggest that you just haven't tried the right wines. We have found that lighter styled wines go very well with the subtle and not so subtle flavors incorporated into Mexican styled foods. Oregon Pinot Noir marries well with rich sauces of dried chilies and chocolate known as mole. The fruit of the wine shines in contrast to the slightly bitter character of the sauce. Chilled White Riesling, Gewürztraminer and Müller-Thurgau are lively quaffers and aid in fire control with some of the more piquant dishes. As with other styles of cooking, Chardonnay pairs well with seafood dishes. The Chardonnay should be of a lighter style without heavy influences of oak or sur-lies aging. The following recipes are my personal favorites. They are quite simple and provide some intriguing wine matches. Salud!

Pavo (Turkey) Mole Rojo

For the Mole Sauce:

10 whole dried Ancho chilies,
    stemmed and seeded
8 whole dried California chilies,
    stemmed and seeded
8 whole dried Pasilla chilies, stemmed
    and seeded
1/2 cup dried currants OR raisins
6 tomatillos, husked and washed
6 Roma tomatoes
1/2 cup sesame seeds, toasted
2 corn tortillas, dried and chopped
8 cloves garlic, minced
2 cups chicken stock
2 teaspoons cinnamon
1 teaspoon pepper
1 teaspoon salt
1/2 teaspoon allspice
1/8 teaspoon Mexican saffron
3 ounces Mexican Ibarra chocolate
2 ounces unsweetened chocolate
3 tablespoons grapeseed oil
    OR peanut oil

Roast the chilies over a gas flame or in a 400 degree oven. Soak chilies in hot water for about 1 hour to rehydrate them, then drain and set aside. Soak currants in hot water for about 30 minutes to rehydrate them, then drain and set aside. Take the whole tomatillos and tomatoes and blacken them all over in a hot skillet.

Place tomatillos, tomatoes, sesame seeds and tortillas in the bowl of a food processor and process until a smooth paste is formed. Add reserved chilies, currants, garlic, chicken stock, pepper, salt, allspice, and saffron and puree together. Melt the chocolates together over low heat, then blend into mixture.

In a cast-iron Dutch oven, heat oil until it just starts to smoke. Carefully add the sauce and reduce heat to medium. Simmer sauce, stirring constantly, for about 10 minutes. Strain through a medium fine sieve. Yields about 1 quart. Sauce can be frozen for future use.

For the Turkey:

2-1/2 pounds turkey meat, cubed
1/2 cup milk
2 tablespoons chili powder
1 teaspoon dried sage
1 tablespoon grapeseed oil
    OR peanut oil

Soak cubed turkey in milk for 30 minutes. Drain and discard milk. Dust meat with chili powder and sage. Heat oil in a large skillet or Dutch oven over medium heat and sauté meat until lightly browned on all sides. Add 2 cups of Mole Sauce and reduce heat to low. Simmer for about 1 hour or until turkey is very tender. Makes 6 servings.

Chilies Rellenos Linda

2 cups water
6 Roma tomatoes
6 tomatillos, husked and washed
1 jalapeño pepper, seeded and minced
1 pound Cheddar cheese
1 pound Monterey Jack cheese
12 fresh Anaheim chilies, roasted and
    peeled
3 eggs, well beaten
1 cup masa harina
3 tablespoons grapeseed oil

Preheat oven to 325 degrees. Lightly oil a large baking dish.

Bring water to a boil in a medium sauce pan. Add whole tomatoes and tomatillos and simmer until tender. Remove from water and remove peels. Discard water. Place skinned tomatoes, tomatillos and jalapeño in the bowl of a food processor and process until a medium consistency is achieved. Slice 1/2-pound of both cheeses. Make a slit in the Anaheim chilies and stuff the cheese inside. Dip the stuffed chilies in the beaten egg, then in the masa harina. Heat oil in a large sauté pan over medium-high heat. Sauté the stuffed chilies until golden on all sides. Place a 1/2 of the tomato mixture in the bottom of prepared baking dish. Lay the chilies in one layer on top, then cover with remaining tomato mixture. Grate remaining cheese and sprinkle on top. Bake for about 45 minutes or until hot and bubbly. Serves 6.

Tequila Lime Shrimp

1 cup Tequila
Juice of 2 limes
1 Serrano chili, seeded and minced
3 cloves garlic, minced
3 tablespoons minced fresh cilantro
1 pound large shrimp (30 to 35 count),
    shelled and deveined

In a large glass mixing bowl, whisk together Tequila, lime juice, chili, garlic and cilantro. Add shrimp and marinate for at least 1 hour, turning occasionally. Thread onto skewers and grill until shrimp are just done. Serve with Susan's Mango Salsa. Serves 6.

Susan's Mango Salsa

1 large ripe mango, peeled and diced
1 red bell pepper, seeded and diced
1 small jalapeño pepper, seeded and
    minced
1/2 cup minced fresh cilantro
1/4 cup olive oil
Juice of 2 limes
Salt and pepper to taste

Place mango, bell pepper, jalapeño and cilantro in a glass or ceramic bowl. In a separate bowl whisk together olive oil and lime juice. Pour over the mango mixture and toss together. Season with salt and pepper. Allow to stand at room temperature for 1 hour to allow flavors to marry. Makes about 1-1/2 pints.

Menu

SUMMER SUNSET
BARBECUE

Tualatin Vineyards Chardonnay
**Grilled Oysters
in the Shell
with Lemon Herb Butter**

Tualatin Vineyards Sauvignon Blanc
**Greek Style
Pasta Salad**

Tualatin Vineyards Pinot Noir
**Rosemary and Garlic
Grilled Lamb Chops**

**Mediterranean Grilled
Vegetable Kabobs**

**Fresh Green Bean Salad
with Hazelnut Vinaigrette**

**Peach and
Raspberry Tart**

Tualatin Vineyards

Tualatin Vineyards was established in 1973, on an old farm in western Oregon by Bill Fuller, a winemaker from Napa Valley and Bill Malkmus, an investment banker from San Francisco. Their goal was to make world class wines in a new viticultural region. The promise of Oregon was its cool, even growing seasons where premium grapes could ripen to their optimum. After just a few short years, Oregon has been recognized as one of the new premium winemaking regions of the world.

Today Tualatin is a modern, 15,000 case, award-winning winery. Its 85 acres of hillside vineyards produce quality estate bottled wines. A lovely tasting room and picnic area offer a spectacular view of the Willamette Valley.

Tualatin's winemaking philosophy is much like its name (Tu-wal-a-tin), the Indian word meaning "gentle and easy flowing." It takes time, patience and care to make wines of great quality. Since 1973, Tualatin has received numerous accolades for its wines including over 60 gold and silver medals in regional, national and international competitions. The highlight was in 1984 when Tualatin 1980 Pinot Noir won the John Sutcliff Trophy, and its 1981 Chardonnay won the Robert Mondovi Trophy for the best of variety at the International Wine and Spirits Competition in London, England. It was the first time that any winery had won trophies for two different wine varieties.

Loving care and personal attention to quality are emphasized in every step of the winemaking process, from the vineyard, to the winery, to the marketplace. Time honored practices of winemaking are complimented by advances in modern technology.

Tualatin's Chardonnays are fermented and aged in traditional small French oak barrels. The wines are left on the lees for up to nine months before bottling to add complexity and richness.

Pinot Noirs are fermented in traditional open redwood tanks to add fruit and varietal flavors. They are also aged in small French oak barrels for up to a year before bottling.

Stainless steel tanks and cool fermentation methods are used to preserve the fragrance and delicate character of the White Riesling, Gewürztraminer and Pinot Noir Blanc. These wines are usually released in the spring while they are still light, young and fresh.

In addition, Tualatin also produces limited quantities of Sauvignon Blanc, Müller-Thurgau and Flora, which are generally available only at the winery.

Grilled Oysters in the Shell with Lemon Herb Butter

1/2 pound butter
1/2 cup Tualatin Vineyards Sauvignon Blanc
Juice and zest of 1 lemon
2 tablespoons minced fresh thyme
2 cloves garlic, minced
1 teaspoon freshly ground pepper
1/2 teaspoon red pepper flakes
32 to 40 medium oysters in the shell, well scrubbed to remove sand and grit
French Bread

Melt butter in a medium sauce pan over low heat. Add Tualatin Vineyards Sauvignon Blanc, lemon juice and zest, thyme, garlic, pepper and red pepper flakes. Simmer for about 10 to 15 minutes.

Place oysters on hot grill. Cook for about 10 to 15 minutes or until liquid begins to bubble on the edge of the shells. Using an oyster knife, pry the shells open and remove oyster. Dip into warm Lemon Herb Butter. Dip French bread into Lemon Herb Butter. Enjoy! Serves 8.

Greek Style Pasta Salad

8 cups cooked bow tie pasta
2 cups cherry tomatoes, halved
1 cup black olives, halved
1 cup pickled peppercinis, seeded and sliced
1 red onion, coarsely chopped
1 medium cucumber, peeled, seeded and sliced
3 tablespoons capers, drained
4 ounces Feta cheese, crumbled

For the Dressing:

1/2 cup olive oil
1/2 cup white wine vinegar
Juice of 1 lemon
1 teaspoon lemon zest
2 cloves garlic, minced
1/2 teaspoon oregano
1/2 teaspoon black pepper
1/2 teaspoon salt

Place Pasta Salad ingredients in a large bowl. Whisk together Dressing ingredients and pour over salad. Toss lightly. Cover and refrigerate overnight, tossing occasionally to distribute dressing. Serves 8.

Wine that maketh glad
the heart of man.
THE BIBLE

Rosemary and Garlic Grilled Lamb Chops

8 lamb chops

For the Marinade:

2 cups Tualatin Vineyards Pinot Noir
1/4 cup olive oil
1/4 cup red wine vinegar
1/4 cup fresh rosemary leaves
2 tablespoons stone-ground Dijon
*   mustard*
1/2 teaspoon cracked black pepper
1/2 teaspoon salt

Place lamb chops in a shallow non-reactive dish or gallon-sized zip-lock type bag. Whisk together marinade ingredients and pour over meat. Refrigerate overnight, turning occasionally.

Grill over hot coals until medium-rare. Serves 8.

Mediterranean Grilled Vegetable Kabobs

For the Basting Sauce:

1/2 cup olive oil
4 cloves garlic, minced
1 tablespoon minced fresh basil
1 tablespoon minced fresh oregano
1/4 teaspoon red pepper flakes
Freshly ground pepper to taste

Combine all ingredients in a small saucepan and simmer over low heat for 30 minutes. Remove from heat and cool.

For the Kabobs:

2 small zucchini, cut into 8 pieces
2 yellow bell peppers, cut into 8 pieces
8 large cherry tomatoes
8 large mushrooms
1 large red onion, quartered
8 small red potatoes, steamed
*   until tender*

Thread one piece of each vegetable onto 8 skewers. Grill over hot coals for about 20 minutes, brushing with Basting Sauce often. Serves 8.

Fresh Green Bean Salad with Hazelnut Vinaigrette

*2 pounds fresh thin green beans,
ends snipped*

Place green beans in a large pot of boiling water and cook 4 to 5 minutes. Drain beans and plunge into ice water to stop the cooking. Drain well and place in a large bowl.

Hazelnut Vinaigrette:

*1/2 cup tarragon-flavored white
wine vinegar*
1/2 cup finely chopped hazelnuts
*1 tablespoon stone-ground Dijon
mustard*
1 tablespoon sugar
1 teaspoon tarragon
1 teaspoon freshly ground black pepper
1 teaspoon salt
Red onion rings to garnish

Whisk together the Hazelnut Vinaigrette ingredients and pour over beans. Toss well. Refrigerate at least 2 hours, tossing occasionally to distribute dressing. Garnish with red onion rings and serve. Serves 8.

Peach and Raspberry Tart

*2 pounds ripe peaches, peeled,
stoned and thinly sliced*
1 pint raspberries
2 tablespoons brandy
1 cup sugar
2 tablespoons cornstarch
2 tablespoons grated orange peel
1/2 teaspoon cinnamon
1 10-inch unbaked pastry shell

Preheat oven to 350 degrees.

Combine peaches, raspberries and brandy in a large bowl. Mix together sugar, cornstarch and cinnamon with a fork and pour over peach mixture. Toss gently to coat. Pour mixture into tart shell and bake for 30 to 40 minutes or until crust is golden brown and fruit is tender. Cool to room temperature. Serves 8.

A Book of Verses underneath the Bough,
A Jug of Wine, a Loaf of Bread—and Thou
Beside me singing in the wilderness—
Oh, Wilderness were Paradise enow!

OMAR KHAYYÁM

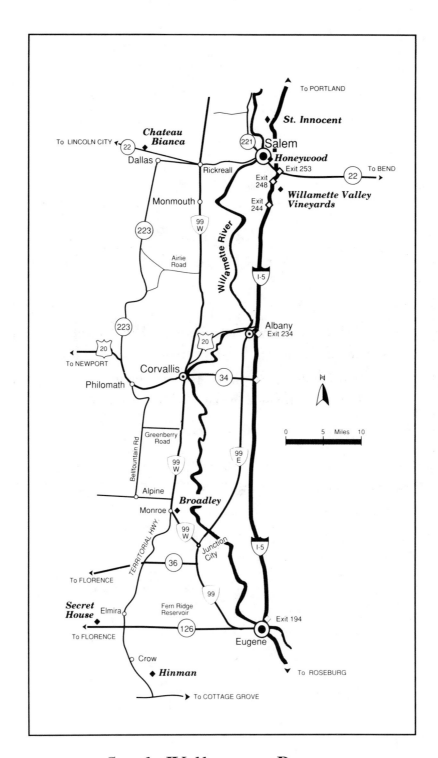

South Willamette Region

South Willamette Region

Menu

SUNDAY DINNER

Broadley Vineyards Chardonnay
**Salmon Mousse with
Sour Cream Dill Sauce**

———

*Broadley Vineyards
Pinot Noir Reserve*
Roasted Duck

**Sour Cream
Mashed Potatoes**

**Asparagus
with Lemon Butter**

**Eggplant, Tomato and
Red Onion Gratin**

———

**Blueberry Pie
with Vanilla Ice Cream**

Broadley Vineyards

Craig and Claudia Broadley left San Francisco for Oregon in 1977 in search of favorable soil and climatic conditions that would produce great Pinot Noir. With the goal of producing big, robust, fruity wines, the search led to the area around the town of Monroe, located in the middle of the Willamette Valley. Known as the "banana belt," this area is the warmest, driest micro-climate in the valley. In 1981, the Broadleys purchased 20 acres of the eastern slope of the valley behind the town of Monroe, and over the next few years planted 17 acres in the Pommard and Wadensval clones of Pinot Noir. The vines were trellised in lyre or U-shaped-style, which numerous studies in France and Australia have shown produce the highest quality fruit.

Although Burgundy wines are their model, the Broadleys fully realize that Oregon is a unique wine frontier. They endeavor to make wines that reflect their environment and wines they personally like—big, robust, fruity Pinot Noir.

Their winemaking style is simple and traditional. Using only grapes from their vineyard, they put whole, unstemmed grapes into 500 to 1,000 gallon wooden tanks. To ensure maximum extraction, the fermenting wine is pushed down several times a day for several weeks, after which it is transferred directly into new French Vosges and Nevers oak barrels. The wine remains in barrels for 17 months before bottling. Fourteen hundred cases of Pinot Noir are produced annually. All wines are estate bottled.

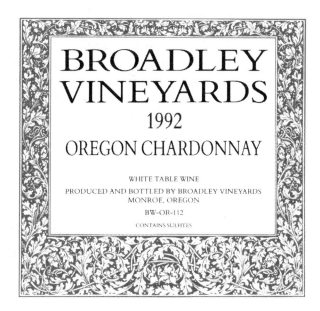

Salmon Mousse with Sour Cream Dill Sauce

For the Salmon Mousse:

1 package unflavored gelatin
1/4 cup cold water
1/2 cup boiling water
1/2 cup mayonnaise
4 tablespoons lemon juice
1 tablespoon grated onion
1 teaspoon salt
1/2 teaspoon Tabasco sauce
1/4 teaspoon paprika
2 cups cooked salmon, finely chopped
1 tablespoon capers, minced
1/2 cup heavy cream
2 cups cottage cheese

Place gelatin and cold water in a large bowl and allow to soften for 10 minutes. Whisk in boiling water and stir until gelatin dissolves. Cool completely. Add mayonnaise, lemon juice, onion, salt, Tabasco and paprika and mix until well blended. Chill until slightly thickened. Add salmon and capers and mix well. Whip the cream until stiff and fold into the mixture. Pour into an oiled 2 quart fish mold. Add cottage cheese to fill the mold. Chill until set. This can be prepared the day before serving. Unmold onto a serving platter and serve with Sour Cream Dill Sauce and toasted French bread. Serves 6.

For the Sour Cream Dill Sauce:

1 egg
2 tablespoons dill weed
4 teaspoons lemon juice
1 teaspoon grated onion
1 teaspoon salt
1/8 teaspoon freshly ground pepper
1-1/2 cups sour cream

Beat egg in a medium bowl until light and lemon colored. Stir in dill weed, lemon juice, onion, salt and pepper. Blend in sour cream until smooth. Chill well before serving.

Roasted Duck

One 4 to 5 pound duck
Salt and pepper
2 tablespoons Broadley Vineyards
    Pinot Noir

Preheat oven to 400 degrees.

Pierce duck all over with a sharp fork. Salt and pepper duck well inside and out. Place a rack in a roasting pan. Place duck on the rack breast side down. Roast for 20 minutes. Remove the duck carefully and place it breast side up on the rack. Pour Broadley Vineyards Pinot Noir over duck. Reduce oven to 350 and continue roasting duck for 1 hour. Remove from oven and allow to sit for 15 minutes before carving. Carve and arrange on a serving platter garnished with watercress. Serves 4.

Sour Cream Mashed Potatoes

5 medium russet potatoes, peeled
    and diced into 3-inch cubes
1/2 cup sour cream
4 tablespoons unsalted butter
Salt and pepper to taste

Fill a large pot with cold water. Place potatoes in pot and bring to a boil. Reduce heat to medium-low and simmer for about 25 minutes or until tender. Drain completely. Return potatoes to pot and add sour cream and butter. Beat with and electric mixer until smooth and fluffy. Season with salt and pepper. Serves 4.

Asparagus with Lemon Butter

1-1/2 pounds asparagus
1/2 cup unsalted butter
3 tablespoons olive oil
1 teaspoon lemon juice
Salt to taste

Trim and discard any tough ends from asparagus. Bring cold, salted water to a boil in a large pot. Add asparagus and boil for 2 minutes. Drain well. Return to the pot and add butter, olive oil, lemon juice and salt. Toss until the asparagus is coated. Serves 4.

Eggplant, Tomato and Red Onion Gratin

Olive oil
1 large eggplant, sliced
2 red onions, sliced
3 to 4 tomatoes, thickly sliced
Salt and pepper to taste

Preheat oven to 350 degrees. Coat the bottom and sides of 2 quart casserole with olive oil.

Put in a layer of eggplant slices, drizzle with olive oil, salt and pepper; then a layer of red onions, drizzle with olive oil, salt and pepper; then top with a layer of tomatoes, drizzle with olive oil, salt and pepper. Bake for about 1 hour. Serves 4.

Blueberry Pie

For the Blueberry Filling:

1 cup sugar
3 tablespoons quick-cooking tapioca
1/2 teaspoon cinnamon
4 to 5 cups blueberries
2 tablespoons butter

Preheat oven to 450 degrees.

Place sugar, tapioca and cinnamon in a medium bowl and stir together with a fork. Add the blueberries and toss to coat. Let stand for 15 minutes.

For the Pie Crust:

1-1/3 cups flour
1 teaspoon salt
1/2 cup cold unsalted butter,
*   cut into small pieces*
1/4 cup ice water

Place flour and salt in the bowl of a food processor. Add the butter and process until mixture resembles coarse meal, about 5 to 10 seconds. With the machine running, pour in the water in steady stream. As soon as the dough comes together in a ball, turn off the machine and remove the dough. Divide the dough into two balls, flatten slightly and chill.

Roll out the dough on a lightly floured board. Fit into a pie plate and prick all over with a fork. Fill with the blueberry filling and dot with butter. Roll out the top crust and fit over pie. Seal the edges together and crimp decoratively. Cut several steam vents in the top crust with a small sharp knife. Bake for 10 minutes at 450 degrees then turn down the oven to 350 degrees and bake an additional 40 to 45 minutes or until golden brown. Serve with vanilla ice cream.

Menu

Of Wine
and Thanksgiving

Chateau Bianca Cuvée Blanc
Spiced Grapes

———

Chateau Bianca Gewürztraminer
Salad with
Basil Oil Dressing
and Homemade Croutons

Roast Turkey with
Gewürztraminer Stuffing
and Wine Gravy

Cranberry and
Golden Raisin Chutney

Garlic
Mashed Potatoes

Acorn Squash Rings

Buttermilk Biscuits

———

Chateau Bianca Pinot Noir
Pears Poached in
Pinot Noir

Chateau Bianca

Chateau Bianca winery was first conceived as a family operation in the mid-1980's. In 1987, the first production was begun to allow for a product that would be salable in the winery's tasting room which was completed in 1991. As is typical of most small Oregon wineries, annual production is very small but committed to high quality. Types of wine currently bottled are: Riesling, Gewürztraminer, Pinot Noir, Chardonnay, a Blush wine, two types of Champagnes, and a Hot Spiced Wine produced from an old family recipe.

The owners, Helmut and Liselotte Wetzel, operate the winery and vineyard with their two children Andreas and Bianca. The Wetzel family's wine heritage goes back to when Helmut's grandfather was producing wine in the famous wine growing region of Wurzburg, Germany. Both Helmut and Lilo were born and raised in Hamburg, Germany, which is a very big seaport in the northern part of the country. As time went on, he immigrated to the United States and the love of wine never left his mind.

In the early 1970's when the Oregon wine industry was just beginning, the desire to return to the wine industry was achieved when Helmut and several partners opened a winery in Forest Grove. Since then he has been an active participant and watched with pleasure as the industry has grown and developed into what is the quickest growing area for wine grape production in the world.

As demand grows for this family-run operation, production and acreage of the vineyards will be increased as well. The family has plans to grow to a maximum 20,000 cases annual production, so that tight quality controls can be maintained on their wines.

Spiced Grapes

1-3/4 cups sugar
3 envelopes unflavored gelatin
1 quart Chateau Bianca Cuvée Blanc
2 large bunches of grapes

In a large sauce pan, combine sugar and gelatin and mix well. Gradually stir in Chateau Bianca Cuvée Blanc. Stir over medium heat until gelatin dissolves and just comes to a boil. Refrigerate until mixture has cooled but not set, about 2 hours.

Clip grapes into small clusters of about 10 grapes each. Dip clusters into gelatin mixture and place on cookie sheet. Chill until set. If gelatin mixture becomes too set when dipping fruit, stir over low heat until liquefied.

Salad with Basil Oil Dressing and Homemade Croutons

For the Croutons:

2 cups French bread cubes (not too soft)
2/3 cup butter
2 teaspoons dried basil
1/2 teaspoon garlic powder
1/2 teaspoon salt
1/4 teaspoon pepper

In a large sauce pan, melt butter over medium heat. When hot, add bread cubes and toss. Add basil, garlic powder, salt and pepper. Continue to toss together until bread is golden. Remove croutons with a slotted spoon and drain on paper towels. Set aside.

For the Salad & Dressing:

2 large heads butter lettuce
6 tablespoons oil
2 tablespoons minced fresh basil
1-1/2 tablespoons Chateau Bianca
  Gewürztraminer
1 large clove garlic, minced
1/2 cup Monterey Jack cheese, grated

Wash and dry lettuce. Tear into bite-sized pieces and refrigerate. In a small bowl, whisk together oil, basil, Chateau Bianca Gewürztraminer, and garlic. Pour dressing over lettuce and toss. Sprinkle with cheese and reserved croutons and toss again. Serve immediately.

Roast Turkey with Basil and Gewürztraminer

1 16-pound turkey
Salt and pepper to taste
Gewürztraminer Stuffing, page 94
6 fresh basil leaves
1 cup Chateau Bianca
Gewürztraminer
2 cups chicken stock
1/2 cup water
1/4 pound butter, melted

Preheat oven to 425 degrees.

Season turkey inside and out with salt and pepper. Spoon Gewürztraminer Stuffing loosely into the turkey and main cavity. Skewer and truss turkey.

With your hand, gently pull the turkey skin away from the breast meat and rub meat with 4 tablespoons of wine. Place three basil leaves in a pretty pattern under the skin on each side of the cavity.

Fill a basting syringe with the remaining wine and inject into various areas of the meat, (the wine will give the meat a wonderful flavor and tenderize it also).

Place turkey on a rack set into a large roasting pan. Pour stock and water into roasting pan. Baste turkey often with the melted butter. Roast turkey for 45 minutes. Reduce temperature to 350 degrees. Cover turkey with foil and continue roasting until meat thermometer inserted into the thickest part of the thigh registers 175 degrees, approximately 2 hours and 15 minutes. Add more water to the pan if drippings get too dry. Skim fat from drippings and reserve 3 tablespoons for the gravy.

Wine Gravy

Turkey neck plus giblets
1 or 2 turkey wings
1 rib celery
1 carrot, peeled
1 small onion, peeled and cut in half
2 whole cloves
1 bay leaf
2 or 3 large parsley sprigs
1-1/2 cups chicken stock
1-1/2 cups Chateau Bianca
Gewürztraminer
1/2 cup Chateau Bianca
Gewürztraminer
Salt and pepper to taste
3 tablespoons turkey fat
3 tablespoons flour

Put the giblets and wings in a sauce pan. Break the celery and carrot in half and add to sauce pan. Stick a whole clove into each half of onion and add to the sauce pan. Add the bay leaf, parsley, chicken stock and wine. Bring mixture to a boil, then reduce heat to low. Cover and simmer for 2 hours. Strain the stock, which should result in about 2 cups. Reserve the giblets for the Gewürztraminer Stuffing. Return the stock to the sauce pan. Simmer over low heat.

When the turkey is done, remove the turkey to a platter and keep warm. Pour all of the pan juices into a tall, narrow cup and skim off as much fat as possible. Reserve 3 tablespoons of fat and discard the rest of the fat. Pour the pan juices into the stock in the sauce pan. Keep simmering over low heat.

Place turkey roasting pan on the stove over medium-high heat and whisk in 1/2 cup Chateau Bianca Gewürztraminer to deglaze the pan, scraping up any browned bits. Add this to the stock in the sauce pan. Season with salt and pepper and keep simmering over low heat.

In a small separate sauce pan, whisk together the reserved turkey fat and flour. Cook over low heat, whisking constantly, until the raw flour aroma dissipates, about 3 minutes. Add 1/4 cup of the simmering stock mixture and whisk until smooth. Add 1 cup of stock mixture and whisk until smooth. Return mixture to sauce pan and cook over medium heat, whisking constantly, until thickened. Gravy should be the consistency of heavy cream.

Gewürztraminer Stuffing

1/3 cup butter
4 tablespoons chopped onion
Reserved turkey giblets, chopped
4 cups cubed raisin bread, lightly
    toasted
1/4 cup Chateau Bianca
    Gewürztraminer
1/4 cup minced fresh parsley
1 tablespoon minced fresh basil
1/4 teaspoon paprika
1/4 teaspoon salt
1/8 teaspoon nutmeg
4 ounces chopped apple
4 ounces chopped celery
4 ounces raisins

Melt butter in a large skillet over medium heat. Add onion and sauté until fragrant. Reduce heat to low and add giblets, bread cubes, Chateau Bianca Gewürztraminer, parsley, basil, paprika, salt and nutmeg. Simmer for about 15 to 20 minutes stirring often. The mixture should be moist but not mushy. Stir in apple, celery and raisins. Let stuffing cool before stuffing the turkey.

Cranberry and Golden Raisin Chutney

2 cups water
1 cup golden raisins
2 cups sugar
2 tablespoons Chateau Bianca
    Gewürztraminer
1 cup freshly squeezed orange juice
2 tablespoons orange zest
2 tablespoons fresh ginger, minced
2 13-ounce packages cranberries
2 small pears, peeled, cored and diced
1 cup slivered almonds, toasted

Bring water to a boil in a large sauce pan. Add raisins. Remove from heat and let stand for 15 minutes. Drain and reserve 1/2 cup water and raisins. Return reserved 1/2 cup water to sauce pan. Add sugar and wine and cook over medium-low heat until sugar dissolves. Increase heat to high and boil without stirring until syrup turns golden brown. Remove from heat. Stir in orange juice, orange zest and ginger until smooth. Add cranberries and cook over medium heat until cranberries begin to pop, about 5 minutes. Stir in reserved raisins, pears and almonds and cook for 1 or 2 minutes. Remove from heat and cool. Cover and refrigerate Cranberry and Golden Raisin Chutney until well chilled.

Garlic Mashed Potatoes

4 pounds baking potatoes, peeled
    and quartered
36 cloves garlic, peeled
9 tablespoons half and half
6 tablespoons butter,
    room temperature
Salt and freshly ground pepper
    to taste
Minced fresh Italian parsley

Combine potatoes and garlic in a large pot and cover with water. Bring to a boil, then reduce heat to medium and cook until potatoes are tender, about 30 minutes. Drain and mash potatoes together with garlic until smooth. Stir in half and half, and butter. Season with salt and pepper. Garnish with minced parsley and serve.

Acorn Squash Rings

2 acorn squash, (1 pound each),
    top and bottom cut off
Salt and pepper to taste
1 tablespoon unsalted butter, melted
1-1/2 tablespoons pure maple syrup
Ground nutmeg to taste

Cut each squash crosswise into 1/2-inch thick slices. Remove seeds from the center. Overlap squash rings slightly in a buttered 13-inch by 9-inch microwave-safe dish. Sprinkle with salt and pepper. Cover dish with plastic wrap. Cook in microwave on high until tender, about 8 minutes. Transfer squash onto a broiler-safe pan. Brush with melted butter and maple syrup. Broil squash rings in preheated broiler about 3-inches from heat source until glazed. Sprinkle with nutmeg. Serve immediately.

Buttermilk Biscuits

2 cups flour
1 tablespoon baking powder
1 teaspoon sugar
1 teaspoon thyme
1/2 teaspoon ginger
1/4 teaspoon baking soda
1/4 teaspoon nutmeg
1/4 teaspoon salt
Freshly ground pepper to taste
5 tablespoons shortening
2 tablespoons minced green bell pepper
3/4 cup buttermilk
    OR 3/4 cup milk with
    1 tablespoon lemon juice
Melted butter

Preheat oven to 425 degrees.

In a large bowl, stir together flour, baking powder, sugar, thyme, ginger, baking soda, nutmeg, salt and pepper until well blended. Cut in the shortening with two knives until mixture resembles coarse meal. Stir in green pepper. Stir in buttermilk until dough holds together. Gather dough into a ball and turn out onto a lightly floured surface. Knead dough lightly, two or three strokes. Pat dough into a rectangle 3/4-inch thick. Using a 2-inch round cookie cutter, cut out about 30 circles. Gather scraps of dough and cut more circles until all dough is used. Place biscuit circles about 2-inches apart on baking sheets. Brush tops with melted butter. Bake for about 12 minutes, or until golden brown.

Pears Poached in Pinot Noir

3 cups Chateau Bianca Pinot Noir
1 cup sugar
1 cinnamon stick, broken into 4 pieces
1/2 vanilla bean OR 2 teaspoons
    vanilla extract
3 whole cloves
3 firm, ripe pears, peeled
6 sprigs fresh mint

Place wine, sugar, cinnamon, vanilla, and cloves in a large sauce pan and bring to a boil. Reduce heat to medium and add pears. Simmer, turning occasionally, until tender but not mushy, about 15 minutes. Transfer pears and syrup to a large bowl. Refrigerate until thoroughly chilled, about 4 hours.

Cut pears in half lengthwise and remove cores. Make several slices lengthwise from stem to base. Transfer a half of a pear onto six plates and place core side down. Press gently to fan slices. Drizzle pears with syrup and garnish with a sprig of mint.

Menu

A HEARTY FIRESIDE DINNER

Hinman Vineyards Pinot Gris
Baked Brie with Pecans

———

Hinman Vineyards Silvan Ridge Pinot Noir
Tossed Green Salad with Balsamic Vinaigrette

Braised Lamb with Juniper and New Potatoes

———

Hinman Vineyards Silvan Ridge Muscat Huxelrebe
Gingered Cheesecake

Hinman Vineyards

Since its inception in 1979 as one of a handful of young Oregon wineries, Hinman has matured into one of the state's top wineries, pointedly announcing its ascendance through the ranks in 1988, when Hinman became the top selling winery in the state. Today, with a production of nearly 35,000 cases a year, Hinman is one of Oregon's largest wineries.

In late August of 1991, Joe Dobbes was hired as winemaker. He brought with him a lifetime of dedication to wine and a world of experience in the fine art of winemaking. Joe worked alongside the best winemakers in Burgundy and Germany, and his ability is reflected in the quality of his wines. In his first years at the winery, Hinman's Pinot Noir, Pinot Gris, and White Riesling all won gold medals at the Oregon State Fair. The success set the tone for a string of further accolades and awards.

In November of 1993, Hinman Vineyards released its brand of reserve wines under the Silvan Ridge label. Through careful vineyard cultivation and management, vinification of small separate lots, and meticulous blending, the goal of rich, elegant, and well balanced wines is magnificently realized. Silvan Ridge wines embody the unique reserve quality expected of limited bottlings.

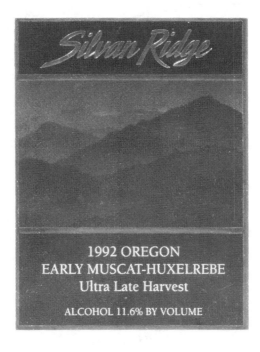

Baked Brie with Pecans

1 8-ounce wheel of Brie cheese
3/4 cup brown sugar
1 cup chopped pecans

Preheat broiler.

Cut off the top rind of Brie. Spread the brown sugar over the top. Press pecans into the brown sugar. Place Brie on a baking sheet and broil for a few minutes, watching for the brown sugar to melt. Remove from oven and place on a serving plate. Serve with Baguette slices. Serves 8.

Tossed Green Salad with Balsamic Vinaigrette

8 cups assorted greens, washed, dried
    and torn into bite-sized pieces
1/2 cup olive oil
1/4 cup Balsamic vinegar
1 teaspoon mayonnaise
2 cloves garlic, minced
1 cup freshly grated Romano cheese

Place greens in a large bowl. In a separate bowl, whisk together olive oil, Balsamic vinegar, mayonnaise and garlic. Pour over greens. Sprinkle Romano over salad and toss well. Serves 8.

Braised Lamb with Juniper and New Potatoes

My favorite meals are one dish wonders—uncomplicated, warm, inviting—a pleasant contrast to the cool, wet Oregon winters.

3 tablespoons olive oil
1 6-pound lamb shoulder, cut into
    stew-sized pieces
2 cups Hinman Vineyards
    Silvan Ridge Pinot Noir
1 cup coarsely chopped onion
1/2 cup coarsely chopped carrot
1/2 cup coarsely chopped celery
3 cloves garlic, minced
2-1/2 teaspoons juniper berries,
    slightly crushed
1 fresh rosemary sprig
    OR 1 teaspoon dry rosemary
Salt and pepper to taste
3 pounds new potatoes, well scrubbed

Heat olive oil in a large enameled iron casserole over medium heat. Add lamb and brown well. Add Hinman Vineyards Silvan Ridge Pinot Noir, onion, carrot, celery, garlic, juniper, rosemary, salt and pepper. Cover and reduce heat to low. Simmer for about 2 hours, stirring every 30 minutes. Add potatoes and turn to coat in liquid. Cover, leaving lid slightly askance, and cook an additional 1-1/2 hours, or until meat and potatoes are very tender and liquid has reduced. Skim off fat and serve immediately. Serve with crusty French bread. Serves 8.

Gingered Cheesecake

For the Crust:

2 cups finely crushed gingersnap
    cookies
5 tablespoons butter
2 tablespoons honey

Preheat oven to 350 degrees.

Melt butter and 2 tablespoons honey together. Add gingersnap crumbs and mix well. Press firmly into the bottom of a 10-inch springform pan.

For the Filling:

11 ounces cream cheese
1/3 cup sugar
2 eggs
1/2 teaspoon vanilla extract

Place cream cheese, 1/3 cup sugar, eggs and 1/2 teaspoon vanilla extract in a medium bowl and mix with an electric mixer until well blended. Pour into prepared springform pan and bake for 20 minutes, or until set. Remove from oven and cool 20 minutes.

For the Topping:

1 cup sour cream
1/4 cup sugar
1/4 teaspoon vanilla extract

Place sour cream, 1/4 cup sugar and 1/4 teaspoon vanilla extract in a bowl and blend. Spread topping on cooled cheesecake. Increase oven temperature to 450 degrees. Bake an additional 8 minutes. Remove from oven and allow cheesecake to cool completely.

For the Glaze:

3/4 cup freshly squeezed
    orange juice
2 tablespoons cornstarch
2 tablespoons honey
1/4 teaspoon grated orange zest
1 small can mandarin orange
    sections, drained

In a small sauce pan, whisk together orange juice and cornstarch. Cook over medium heat, whisking constantly, until thick and glossy, about 7 to 10 minutes. Remove from heat and whisk in 2 tablespoons honey and orange zest. Stir in mandarin slices. Pour over cheesecake and chill thoroughly, at least 6 hours. Serves 8.

And Noah he often said to his wife
when he sat down to dine,
"I don't care where the water goes
if it doesn't get into the wine."

CHESTERTON

99

Menu

A Winery Supper for Friends

Honeywood Pinot Noir
Meatballs in
Cranberry and
Pinot Noir Sauce

Honeywood Gooseberry Wine
Halibut in
Gooseberry Wine Sauce

Steamed
New Potatoes

Broccoli
with Lemon Butter

Honeywood Blackberry Wine
Blackberry Wine
Raisin Cake

Honeywood Winery

In 1933, Honeywood Winery was founded by Ron Honeyman and John Wood. It was originally called Columbia Distilleries, and produced fruit brandies, cordials and liqueurs.

Eventually, they settled on making premium fruit wines and decided a name change was in order for the winery. Contrary to the obvious, Messrs. Honeyman and Wood did not use a contraction of their names to make Honeywood, and in fact, objected to the name on those grounds. An advertising consultant, who knew a good thing when he saw it, provided the rationale with a line from Oliver Goldsmith's play, *The Good Natured Man*, wherein the products of fermentation were referred to as, "smooth as HONEY. . . aged in WOOD. . . the drink of a good-natured man." By coincidence or design, Honeywood became synonymous with the elite in wines.

Obviously, a winery must be close to its source of ingredients, and so it is with Honeywood. Located in Salem, in the heart of Oregon's great and fertile Willamette Valley, the winery is minutes away from some of the world's finest vineyards, cane berry fields and fruit orchards.

Since 1982, the winery has produced fine varietal wines from the winery's casks now come light, zesty, fresh wines that capture the fruitiness and varietal character of the grape. Honeywood by design does not have a vineyard, choosing instead to emphasize the wine-making process. It buys grapes under contract from local growers, setting high standards, and with the right under the contract to reject bad fruit, maintains the highest standards possible. Grapes are purchased primarily from growers in the Willamette Valley, an area similar to the classic vineyard regions of France and Germany, being well suited to white wines and the red Pinot Noir. Acres of rich volcanic soil, abundant water, and ideal growing conditions with long days of summer and clement winters, are a combination that produce wines of full varietal character and good acid balance. This relatively new wine region, protected from the maritime influence of the Pacific Ocean by the Coastal Range and from the extremes of continental weather by the Cascades, produces some of the finest world-class wines anywhere.

While the grape throughout the centuries has held top echelon position as the best known ingredient for wine, all fruits and berries produce an equally delightful potion. It follows then, that the wines from fruits can be as varied in character as the skill of the winemaker and the varieties of fruit available to him. There is an optimum time, when the sugar content is just right and berries, at their prime of maturity, must be harvested. This means buying fruits in the fields and on the trees. It means that fresh fruit for juice to start the vinting process is never overripe, and just sweet enough. Without that care, you'd have just another fruit wine. As it is you have Honeywood fine fruit wines.

Meatballs in Cranberry and Pinot Noir Sauce

For the Cranberry and Pinot Noir Sauce:

1 16-ounce can whole cranberry sauce
1 cup brown sugar
1/2 cup Honeywood Pinot Noir
2 teaspoons prepared mustard

Preheat oven to 375 degrees. Lightly oil a shallow baking dish.

Stir together all Cranberry and Pinot Noir Sauce ingredients in a medium sauce pan. Simmer over medium heat for 5 minutes, stirring often. Remove from heat and set aside until needed.

For the Meatballs:

2 pounds lean ground beef
1-1/2 cups fresh bread crumbs
1/2 cup finely chopped celery
1/2 cup finely chopped onion
2 eggs
1 tablespoon Worcestershire sauce
2 teaspoons garlic salt
1/4 teaspoon pepper

Combine all meatball ingredients in a large bowl and mix well. Shape into 24 1-1/2-inch balls. Place in one layer in baking dish. Bake for 20 minutes. Pour Cranberry and Pinot Noir Sauce over and bake an additional 15 minutes. Remove to a serving platter and serve. Serves 4.

Halibut in Gooseberry Wine Sauce

This recipe was developed by Chef Sean Robinson, Regrade's Restaurant, in Seattle, Washington.

1 tablespoon butter
4 6-ounce halibut steaks
Salt and white pepper to taste
1/4 cup Honeywood Gooseberry Wine

Preheat oven to 350 degrees. Butter a shallow baking dish large enough to hold fish in one layer. Place fish in dish and season with salt and white pepper. Pour in 1/4 cup Honeywood Gooseberry Wine. Bake for 10 to 15 minutes, depending on thickness of halibut. Remove halibut from oven and place on serving platter. Ladle Gooseberry Wine Sauce over each piece. Serves 4.

For the Gooseberry Sauce:

1/2 cup Honeywood Gooseberry Wine
1/4 cup shallots, minced
1/4 cup heavy cream
3 tablespoons cold butter,
 cut into pieces

Combine 1/2 cup Honeywood Gooseberry Wine and shallots in a heavy sauce pan. Reduce mixture to 2 tablespoons over medium heat, being careful not to burn mixture. Add cream and reduce to 1/4 cup. Remove from heat and whisk in butter a little at a time, incorporating each bit before adding another. Sauce should be slightly tart.

Steamed New Potatoes

12 small new potatoes
Minced fresh parsley

Wash potatoes well. Remove a strip of peel around the center of each potato with a potato peeler and discard strip of peel. Place potatoes in a steaming basket and steam until tender. Place potatoes in a serving bowl and sprinkle with parsley. Serves 4.

Broccoli with Lemon Butter

2 pounds broccoli, trimmed
3 tablespoons butter
2 tablespoons fresh lemon juice

Steam or boil broccoli until tender. Melt butter and lemon juice together in a small sauce pan over low heat. Toss broccoli with lemon butter and serve. Serves 4.

Blackberry Wine Raisin Cake

For the Blackberry Wine Raisin Cake:

2 cups firmly packed brown sugar
3/4 cup butter, at room temperature
2 eggs
3 cups flour
2 teaspoons baking powder
1 teaspoon cinnamon
1/2 teaspoon nutmeg
1/2 teaspoon salt
1 cup Honeywood Blackberry Wine
1 cup raisins
1 cup chopped pecans

Preheat oven to 350 degrees. Butter and flour a bundt pan.

In a large bowl, cream together the brown sugar and butter until fluffy. Beat in eggs. Sift together the flour, baking powder, cinnamon, nutmeg and salt. Add flour mixture and 1 cup Honeywood Blackberry Wine alternately to the creamed mixture, starting and ending with flour mixture, beating well after each addition. Fold in raisins and pecans. Pour batter into prepared bundt pan. Bake for 55 to 60 minutes, or until toothpick inserted in the center comes out clean. Cool for 10 minutes then loosen edges and invert onto a rack to cool completely. Frost with Blackberry Wine Frosting.

For the Blackberry Wine Frosting:

2 cups powdered sugar
1/2 cup butter, at room temperature
2 tablespoons Honeywood Blackberry Wine

In a large bowl, cream together the powdered sugar and butter. Beat in the Honeywood Blackberry Wine until frosting is a spreading consistency.

Menu

PASSOVER DINNER FOR 24

Secret House Chardonnay
**Northwest Gefilte Fish Terrine
with Horseradish, Caper
and Tomato Mayonnaise**

Chopped Liver à la Patti's Pâte

Haroseth

Matzo

———

Secret House Pinot Noir
**Roast Leg of Lamb
with Pinot Mustard Marinade**

**Secret
Tabbouleah**

**Steamed Asparagus with
Lemon Sauce**

———

Secret House Late Harvest Riesling
**Late Harvest Riesling Pears
with Raspberry Sauce**

Secret House

Located in the foothills of the Coast Range in Veneta, Secret House Vineyards were planted with Pinot Noir, Riesling, and Chardonnay in 1972. They are a small family-owned winery dedicated to producing premium wines at reasonable prices. The winery welcomes visitors February through December, and an annual wine and blues festival is held there in August.

Every spring I am invited to cook and celebrate Passover with some dearly loved friends of Secret House. Passover is a joyful feast that commemorates the deliverance of the Jewish Tribes from bondage in Egypt. It is also known as the Festival of Unleavened Bread, because in their haste to pack the camels and donkeys with their worldly goods, there was only enough time to prepare unleavened bread (matzo) to take with them.

There is a wonderful group of us from all religions who sing, drink, feast and tell the story of Passover. We all can celebrate the joys of being set free in the springtime and embrace the bountiful year.

Naturally we serve lots of Secret House wine during the dinner. I also try to freeze some Pinot Noir juice during crush for a special grape juice treat.

Northwest Gefilte Fish Terrine with Horseradish, Caper and Tomato Mayonnaise

Never again will they want to forget the gefilte fish. This is divine—it is also a wonderful summer entree with a crisp salad and cold bottle of Secret House Chardonnay.

4 red snapper filets
Cold water
2 large onions, chopped
4 small carrots, peeled and sliced
2 ribs celery, sliced
5 sprigs fresh parsley
1 tablespoon chopped fresh dill
1 tablespoon chopped fresh tarragon
1 pound ling cod OR other
     white-fleshed fish, cut into
     1-inch cubes
1 pound halibut OR other
     white-fleshed fish, cut into
     1-inch cubes
3 eggs
1/2 cup cold water
Salt and freshly ground black pepper
     to taste
1-1/2 pounds Chinook salmon filet,
     cut into 1/2-inch cubes

Preheat oven to 350 degrees. Lightly oil a 2-quart baking dish, line it with wax paper and lightly oil the wax paper.

Soak red snapper filets in cold water for 10 minutes. Drain and pat dry. Discard water. Place red snapper filets in between wax paper and flatten slightly with a mallet or heavy side of a knife. Line prepared baking dish with red snapper, slightly overlapping. Cover with plastic wrap and refrigerate 45 minutes.

Place onions, carrots, celery, parsley, dill and tarragon in the bowl of a food processor and process until smooth. Add ling cod and halibut and pulse until just smooth. Add eggs, one at a time, alternately with 1/2 cup cold water and pulse until smooth. Season to taste with salt and pepper.

Place fish mixture in a large bowl and gently fold in salmon cubes. Spoon the mixture over the red snapper fillets. Cover with oiled wax paper, then a sturdy double layer of foil. Place the terrine in a large baking pan and pour in hot water to come halfway up the sides. Bake for 50 to 60 minutes or until a knife inserted in the center comes out clean. Serve with Horseradish, Caper and Tomato Mayonnaise (recipe on following page). Serves 24 as an appetizer.

Wine comes in at the mouth
And love comes in at the eye;
That's all we shall know for truth
Before we grow old and die.

YEATS

Horseradish, Caper and Tomato Mayonnaise

2 cups mayonnaise
2 tomatoes, seeded and diced
1/2 cup capers
3 green onions (including the
    green part), minced
2 tablespoons grated fresh horseradish
1 tablespoon minced fresh dill
1 tablespoon minced fresh parsley

Combine all ingredients in a small bowl and chill at least 2 hours before serving.

Chopped Liver à la Patti's Pâte

Ever have someone say—"yuck, chicken livers, I wouldn't touch them!" This will convert them into faithful fans. You will get requests for this smooth pâte at all of your social gatherings.

2 pounds fresh chicken livers,
    all membranes removed
1/2 cup brandy
1/4 pound unsalted butter
3 large onions, coarsely chopped
3 cloves garlic, minced
1/2 cup chopped fresh parsley
1-1/2 teaspoons minced fresh thyme
1 teaspoon minced fresh rosemary
2 teaspoons Mrs. Dash salt substitute
    OR salt
2 teaspoons white pepper
1/4 teaspoon cayenne pepper
2 envelopes unflavored gelatin
1 cup cold water
1-3/4 pounds unsalted butter,
    at room temperature

Soak chicken livers in brandy for 15 minutes. Drain and reserve brandy.

Melt 1/4 pound butter in a large skillet over medium heat. Add onions and garlic and sauté until transparent. Add chicken livers and sauté until cooked but still pink inside, about 10 minutes. Add brandy to pan and flame. Add parsley, thyme, rosemary, Mrs. Dash, white pepper and cayenne and remove from heat.

Dissolve gelatin in cold water. Place in the bowl of a food processor along with chicken liver mixture and 1-3/4 pounds butter. Process until smooth. Spoon into a serving bowl and chill until firm. Mixture can also be put in a decorative mold and unmolded when firm. Serve with crackers and cucumber slices. Serves 25 to 35 as an appetizer.

Haroseth

6 cups chopped pitted dates
2 cups chopped raisins
1 cup Secret House Pinot Noir
1 cup Secret House Late Harvest
    Riesling
1 pound finely chopped walnuts
1 tablespoon finely minced fresh ginger

Place the dates, raisins, Secret House Pinot Noir and Secret House Late Harvest Riesling in a large bowl and blend well. Stir in walnuts and ginger and blend well. Shape into a pyramid. Cover with plastic wrap and chill well. Serves 24.

Roast Leg of Lamb with Pinot Mustard Marinade

Marinade:

2/3 cup olive oil
21 cloves garlic, minced
2/3 cup chopped fresh basil
1/3 cup chopped fresh parsley
2 tablespoons minced fresh rosemary
1 tablespoon Cajun spice mix
4 cups Secret House Pinot Noir
1-1/2 cups Dijon mustard
2 tablespoons freshly ground pepper
3 legs of lamb

Heat olive oil in a sauté pan over medium-low heat. Add garlic, basil, parsley, rosemary and Cajun spice and sauté until fragrant. Add Secret House Pinot Noir, mustard and pepper and bring to a simmer. Remove from heat and allow to cool.

Place lamb in three large zip-lock type bags and divide marinade between them. Marinate 24 hours in the refrigerator, turning bags occasionally.

Preheat oven to 500 degrees.

Place lamb in roasting pan and put in oven. Immediately turn oven down to 325 degrees. Roast until a meat thermometer inserted in the thickest part reads 160 degrees. Remove from oven and allow to rest for 15 minutes before carving. Serves 24.

Secret Tabbouleah

7-1/2 cups water
3-1/2 cups bulgar
1-1/2 cups lemon juice
2-1/2 cups olive oil
3-1/2 cups coarsely chopped fresh mint
3-1/3 cups coarsely chopped
    fresh parsley
2 cups finely diced red onion
1/2 cup coarsely chopped fresh basil
2 tablespoons minced garlic
1-1/2 tablespoons freshly ground
    pepper
1-1/2 tablespoons salt
4 cups chopped plum tomatoes
3 cups chopped peeled cucumber

Bring water to a boil in a large pot. Stir in bulgar and return to boil. Cover and reduce heat to low. Simmer until bulgar has absorbed the water, about 20 minutes. Put bulgar in a large bowl and cool.

Whisk together olive oil and lemon juice. Pour over bulgar and toss well. Add remaining ingredients and toss well. Cover and refrigerate overnight to allow flavors to marry. Garnish with fresh mint leaves and cherry tomatoes. Serves 24.

Steamed Asparagus with Lemon Sauce

12 egg yolks
1/2 cup fresh lemon juice
1 teaspoon cayenne pepper
Salt and white pepper to taste
1 pound unsalted butter, melted
    and kept hot

Combine egg yolks, lemon juice, cayenne pepper, salt and white pepper in a food processor and process until smooth. With motor running, add hot butter slowly in a thin stream until emulsified. Transfer to a serving bowl.

9 pounds young asparagus

Steam asparagus until crisp-tender. Drizzle with Lemon Sauce and serve. Serves 24.

How simple and frugal a thing is happiness:
a glass of wine, a roast chestnut,
a wretched little brazier, the sound of the sea.
All that is required to feel
that here and now is happiness
is a simple frugal heart.

KAZANTZAKIS

Late Harvest Riesling Pears with Raspberry Sauce

10 cups water
8 cups sugar
1 bottle Secret House Late Harvest
    Riesling
24 ripe pears, peeled
1 quart fresh raspberries
1 cup Secret House Late Harvest
    Riesling
2 tablespoons cornstarch

Combine water, sugar and 1 bottle Secret House Late Harvest Riesling in a large pot. Bring to a boil and boil for 5 minutes. Reduce heat to medium-low and add pears. Simmer until pears are tender but not mushy, about 5 to 10 minutes. Remove from heat and let pears cool in syrup. Chill.

In a medium sauce pan, combine raspberries, 1 cup Secret House Late Harvest Riesling and cornstarch. Bring to a boil, stirring constantly. Remove from heat. Chill.

To serve, drizzle some of the Raspberry Sauce on plates, top with a poached pear and drizzle a little more Raspberry Sauce over pear. Serves 24.

Menu

MEMORIAL DAY OPEN HOUSE

*St. Innocent Vintage
Méthode Champenois Brut*

*St. Innocent O'Conner
Vineyard Pinot Noir*

*St. Innocent Seven Springs
Vineyard Chardonnay*

———

Herbed Leg
of Lamb

Beans Provencial

———

Chocolate Hazelnut
Torte

Queen Mother's Cake

———

Assorted Cheeses such as:
Brie, Herbed Brie, Jarlsburg,
Havarti and Dilled Havarti

Assorted Breads

St. Innocent Winery

St. Innocent, Ltd. was founded in May, 1988 by winemaker and President Mark Vlossak and eight investors. Ten tons were harvested in the fall of 1988, producing 396 cases of still wine and 176 cases of sparkling wine. Production increased to 4,300 cases in 1994, and we expect to achieve a full capacity of 5,000 cases by the end of this century. It is our intention to produce small lot, handmade still and sparkling wines.

The winery produces vineyard designated Pinot Noir and Chardonnay still wines. St. Innocent owns no vineyards. We work closely with growers owning unique sites producing grapes that have a concentration of flavor that reflects the terroir of that site. The close relationship we have with our growers focuses on fine tuning viticultural techniques to focus these flavor and aroma components. The winery currently produces three single vineyard Pinot Noir and three Chardonnay wines.

A vintage dated Méthode Champenoise sparkling wine has been produced each year since 1988. The base wines are a blend of Pinot Noir and Chardonnay and are lees aged. Malo-lactic fermentation is encouraged and the base wines are generally unrefined. Tirage time is a minimum of three years. We wish to produce a sparkling wine that is complex with elegant flavors and the balances to accompany a variety of foods.

Herbed Leg of Lamb

One 5 to 7 pound leg of lamb,
  boned and butterflied
20 cloves garlic, sliced in half
  lengthwise
1 tablespoon olive oil
1 tablespoon soy sauce
1 teaspoon ginger
1 teaspoon marjoram
1 teaspoon pepper
1 teaspoon rosemary
1 teaspoon sage
1 teaspoon salt
1 teaspoon thyme

Preheat oven to 450 degrees.

Cut small slits in the lamb and insert garlic slivers. Combine olive oil, soy sauce, ginger, marjoram, pepper, rosemary, sage, salt and thyme into a paste. Rub mixture all over and into the meat. Place the meat on a rack in a roasting pan. Brown in the oven for 20 minutes. Reduce oven temperature and roast for 16 minutes per pound for medium, or until a meat thermometer reads 160 degrees. Remove from the oven and let stand for 20 minutes before carving. Reserve all pan juices, including fat, for Beans Provencial (see recipe below). Serves 8.

Drink no longer water,
but use a little wine for thy stomach's sake.

THE BIBLE

Beans Provencial

2 quarts water
2 cups organic small white beans
2 cups water
1 cup strong chicken stock
1 onion
5 whole cloves
5 cloves garlic
2 bay leaves
1 teaspoon salt
Pan juices from lamb
1/2 cup minced parsley

Bring 2 quarts water to a boil in a large pot. Add beans and return to a boil. Remove from heat and allow to sit for 2 hours. Drain beans and discard liquid.

Return beans to pot with 2 cups water, chicken stock, onion stuck with whole cloves, garlic, bay leaves and salt. Simmer over low heat until beans are very tender, adding more water as necessary to keep beans from drying out. When beans are tender, discard onion, cloves, garlic and bay leaves. Stir in pan juices from lamb and parsley. Serves 8.

Chocolate Hazelnut Torte

For the Torte:

12 ounces finely ground hazelnuts
3 tablespoons sifted flour
1 teaspoon baking powder
6 eggs, separated
1-1/2 cups sugar
2 tablespoons instant coffee
2 teaspoons cocoa powder
1/8 teaspoon salt

Preheat oven to 350 degrees. Butter two 9-inch cake pans, line with waxed paper and dust with fine dry, breadcrumbs or flour.

In a medium bowl, mix together the hazelnuts, flour and baking powder.

In another medium bowl, beat egg yolks until lemon colored, then reduce speed and add sugar, instant coffee and cocoa powder. Increase speed and beat on high for 5 minutes until very thick.

Place egg whites and salt in a large bowl and beat until stiff. Carefully fold the yolk mixture into the egg whites. Fold in the nut mixture.

Divide batter into the prepared cake pans and gently level. Bake 35 to 40 minutes or until layers barely pull away from the sides of the pans. Remove from oven and invert onto racks, but do not remove pans for 10 minutes. Then invert and cool completely right side up.

For the Glaze:

1/2 cup heavy cream
2 teaspoons instant coffee
8 ounces semi-sweet OR bittersweet
chocolate, chopped

Place cream in a heavy sauce pan and scald over medium heat. Remove from heat and whisk in the instant coffee. Add the chocolate and whisk until melted. Cool to room temperature and drizzle glaze over the layers. Serve with Pinot Noir or strong coffee.

Queen Mother's Cake

6 ounces semi-sweet chocolate,
  broken up
6 ounces butter
3/4 cup sugar
6 eggs, separated
6 ounces finely ground hazelnuts
1/8 teaspoon salt

Preheat oven to 375 degrees. Butter a 9-inch springform pan, line the bottom with waxed paper and dust with fine dry bread crumbs or flour.

Place chocolate in the top of a double-boiler and melt over barely simmering water. Set aside to cool.

In a large bowl, cream the butter. Add sugar gradually then beat on high for 3 minutes. Add egg yolks one at a time, beating well after each addition. Stir in the cooled chocolate and hazelnuts.

In a separate bowl, beat egg whites and salt until stiff. Carefully fold 1/4 of the egg whites into the yolk mixture. Fold in the remaining egg whites in thirds.

Pour batter into prepared pan and gently level.

Bake for 20 minutes, then reduce heat to 350 degrees and continue baking for an additional 50 minutes. Remove from oven and place on a moist towel for 20 minutes. Remove springform, invert onto a rack and remove pan bottom and waxed paper. Invert again and cool completely right side up. Glaze.

For the Glaze:

1/2 cup heavy cream
2 teaspoons instant coffee
8 ounces semi-sweet OR bittersweet
  chocolate, chopped

Place cream in a heavy sauce pan and scald over medium heat. Remove from heat and whisk in the instant coffee. Add the chocolate and whisk until melted. Cool to room temperature and drizzle glaze over the cake.

Bring water, bring wine, boy!
Bring flower garlands to me!
Yes, bring them, so that I may try a bout
with love.

ANACREON

Pinot Noir

My general approach to Pinot Noir involves handling the fruit in ways that increase the spectrum of fruit flavors while limiting the extraction of harsh tannins and seed or stem components. We destem all of the fruit and try to keep 25% whole berries. The must is pumped directly into fermenters filled with inert gas to minimize oxygen contact. The tank is cooled and the grapes are allowed to 'cold soak' for a period of days. This increases fruit flavor components without extracting harsh tannins. The cooling is stopped and the tank is inoculated with yeast and allowed to ferment to dryness. We punch down by hand once or twice daily. The must is pressed gently and the new wine is allowed to settle in the tank prior to racking into small oak barrels. From this time on handling is kept to a minimum.

Chardonnay

Chardonnay is handled to increase a complex range of flavors derived from the fruit, barrel fermentation and lees aging. We want to keep a balance of all the components without allowing any single facet to dominate the wine. This enhances the interaction of the wine with the food. The fruit is picked very cold (usually less than 50 degrees F.) in the early morning, destemmed, and the must is pumped into large bins to undergo 18 to 24 hours of skin contact. This contact increases fruit flavor and aroma extraction. Keeping the temperature low minimizes the extraction of bitter phenolic compounds. The must is gently pressed and racked to tanks for cooling and settling. The clear juice is pumped into barrels and inoculated with yeast. As fermentation slows, the barrels are topped and the wine is left to age on the yeast lees.

The vineyard lends an identity to a wine that goes beyond the style of an individual winemaker. The term 'terroir' is used to describe the interaction of the soil, exposure, and micro-climate of a vineyard (not to be confused with the term 'terror', which is used to describe the interaction of winemaker, grapegrower, and weather forecasts in the early fall). It results in a complex of flavors that can be identified in the wines from a particular site that were made by different winemakers. A vineyard may have a set of fruit aromas; for example, in Pinot Noir, these may be cherry, raspberry, cassis, as well as spicy or peppery notes. The complex interaction of these aromas and flavors identifies the terroir. The Burgundian varieties, Chardonnay and especially Pinot Noir, are particularly influenced by the terroir on which they are grown. The winemaker has the opportunity to capture those unique flavors in the wine. The consumer has the opportunity to taste something truly unique, flavors beyond the usual blend of grapes.

Menu

A Formal Christmas Dinner

Willamette Valley Vineyards Pinot Gris
Grape and Tuna Stuffed Mushroom Caps

———

Willamette Valley Vineyards White Riesling
Fresh Fruit Cup

———

Willamette Valley Vineyards Chardonnay
Willamette Valley Vineyards
Whole Berry Pinot Noir
**Roast Turkey with
Hazelnut Stuffing and Turkey Gravy**

Cranberry Relish

Candied Sweet Potatoes

Green Beans with Almonds

———

Willamette Valley Vineyards Dry Riesling
Pumpkin Pie Squares

———

*Willamette Valley Vineyards
Gewürztraminer*
*Willamette Valley Vineyards
Pinot Noir Ice Wine*
Mincemeat Pie
Willamette Valley Vineyards Nog

Willamette Valley Vineyards

Willamette Valley Vineyards, located in the heart of the Willamette Valley, is Oregon's premier landmark winery. Since its beginning in 1988, Willamette Valley has created delicious, award-winning wines that have captured the hearts and palates of wine enthusiasts nationwide.

Unique to Oregon, this public company was conceived by local wine enthusiasts united by a dream to develop a beautiful winery and produce wines of exceptional quality. These founders contribute their time and talents to create, share and enjoy the remarkable wines.

The vineyard's red clay soil and micro-climate are similar to the growing conditions of the famous winemaking region of Burgundy, France. The south and southwest facing slopes are ideal for the vine's collection of sunlight. Fresh marine breezes cool the slowly developing grapes, yielding intense fruit flavors. Presently grown on the winery's estate vineyards are Pinot Noir, Chardonnay, Pinot Gris and White Riesling; a total of 55 acres.

The art and science of making grapes into wine is the focus of winemaker Dean Cox. Dean combines state-of-the-art facilities and age-old European methods of cellaring and aging to produce not just good wines, but exceptional ones. With formal winemaking training at University of California Davis and over 12 years experience, his winemaking prowess has rewarded Willamette Valley Vineyards with many highly acclaimed wines.

Working together, with an uncompromising dedication toward quality, the winery's founders believe Oregon can become one of the greatest wine regions in the world; distinct to herself and unique to her environment. Willamette Valley Vineyards invites you to share the Oregon spirit and taste its delicious wines.

Grape and Tuna Stuffed Mushroom Caps

32 large mushrooms
4 tablespoons butter
1 cup Willamette Valley Vineyards
    Dry White Riesling
1 6-1/2-ounce can water-packed tuna,
    well drained
3 hard-cooked eggs, coarsely chopped
1/2 cup seedless green grapes,
    sliced in half
2 tablespoons chopped red onion
1 teaspoon finely grated lemon zest
Freshly ground pepper to taste
3 tablespoons mayonnaise
2 tablespoons sour cream

Preheat oven to 400 degrees.

Clean the mushrooms with a damp cloth. Remove stems and reserve. Place the mushroom caps in a shallow baking dish, in one layer, stem side up. Dot with butter. Pour in Willamette Valley Vineyards Dry White Riesling. Bake for 10 to 15 minutes.

Chop the reserved mushroom stems finely and place in a large bowl. Stir in tuna, eggs, grapes, onion, lemon zest and pepper and toss gently. In a small bowl, blend the mayonnaise and sour cream. Add to the tuna mixture and toss until well combined. Stuff the cooked mushrooms with tuna mixture. Refrigerate until ready to serve, then heat slightly. Serve on a bed of grape leaves and sprinkle a few uncooked cranberries for color. Serves 8.

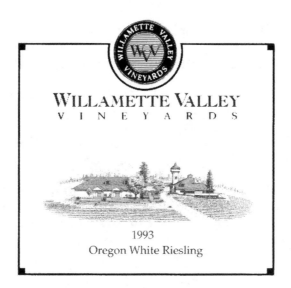

WILLAMETTE VALLEY
V I N E Y A R D S

1993
Oregon White Riesling

Fresh Fruit Cup

Fresh pineapple
Red apples, sliced
Kiwi fruit
Red seedless grapes
White seedless grapes
Banana slices
Orange sections
2 cups orange juice

Remove the pineapple skin, kiwi skin, orange peel and banana peel.

Chunk, dice and slice fruit into bite-sized pieces. Place in a large bowl and pour orange juice over pieces and refrigerate until serving. Serve in short stemmed sorbet glasses garnished with mint leaves. Serves 8.

Roast Turkey with Hazelnut Stuffing and Turkey Gravy

For the Hazelnut Stuffing:

2 tablespoons vegetable oil
3 cups chopped celery with leaves
2 cups chopped onions
2 tart apples, peeled, cored and
*   diced into 1/2-inch cubes*
1 cup hazelnuts, toasted, skinned
*   and chopped*
6 cups stale bread cubes
1 cup Willamette Valley Vineyards
*   Gewürztraminer*
1 cup chicken stock
1 teaspoon dried thyme
1 teaspoon dried sage
1 teaspoon salt
Freshly ground pepper to taste

Heat the oil in a large skillet over low heat. Sauté celery and onions until softened but not browned, about 10 minutes. Transfer to a large mixing bowl. Stir in apples, hazelnuts and bread cubes and toss lightly. In a separate bowl, combine Willamette Valley Vineyards Gewürztraminer, chicken stock, thyme, sage, salt and pepper and stir. Pour over bread mixture and toss until well coated. Refrigerate stuffing until ready to stuff the turkey.

Preheat oven to 325 degrees.

Treat yourself with fresh turkey, it is much more succulent than frozen. Determine the weight by figuring one pound per person. A younger turkey will normally be tenderer.

Remove the giblets and neck from the bird's cavity. Rinse well inside and out and pat dry with paper towels. Refresh the meat inside and out with fresh orange juice.

Loosely fill cavity with about 7 cups of the Hazelnut Stuffing, leaving room for expansion. Fill the neck cavity with 3 cups of the stuffing. Do not stuff the bird until you are ready to cook it.

Roast the bird at 325 degrees, breast side up. Baste at least once an hour with pan juices and butter. Determine doneness by pricking the skin in the thickest part of the thigh; the juices should be clear.

For a bird up to 16 pounds: Stuffed: allow 20 to 25 minutes per pound; Unstuffed: allow 5 minutes per pound.

For a bird over 16 pounds: Stuffed: allow 18 to 20 minutes per pound; Unstuffed: allow 15 minutes per pound.

Remove the turkey to a heated platter, cover loosely and let stand at least 15 minutes. This allows the juices to settle and makes carving easier.

It is suggested to carve the turkey in the kitchen, arrange slices of white then dark meat on a platter. Garnish the platter with fresh mint, placing the turkey on a bed of mint.

For the Turkey Gravy:

Turkey giblets
8 cups water
1/2 cup flour
Pan juices left from cooking
*   the turkey*

Place the giblets and water in a medium sauce pan. Simmer over low heat for about 1 hour. Remove the giblets and chop them coarsely. Reserve the cooking broth.

Remove turkey from roasting pan. Remove about half of the excess fat from the pan and discard. Place roasting pan on the stove burner over medium heat. Whisk in the flour until smooth. Cook the flour and juices together for 3 minutes, whisking constantly. Add reserved giblet broth slowly, whisking constantly. Continue whisking until desired consistency is achieved. Add cooked, chopped giblets if desired. Season to taste. Serve in a gravy boat.

Cranberry Relish

*1 pound fresh cranberries (4 cups),
    washed and picked over*
2 thin-skinned seedless oranges
2 tart apples, cored and quartered
1/3 lemon with peel
1 cup finely chopped celery
1/2 cup walnuts, chopped
2 cups sugar

Grind the cranberries, oranges, apples and lemon together, including their skins. Stir in the celery and walnuts. Stir in the sugar. Place the mixture in a covered jar and refrigerate. Allow the relish to ripen for two days before serving.

This is served nicely in a relish dish lined with fresh, crisp lettuce leaves, with the relish spooned on top.

Candied Sweet Potatoes

*3 pounds sweet potatoes, peeled
    and sliced into 1/2-inch rounds*
3/4 cup brown sugar
3 tablespoons unsalted butter
2 tablespoons water
1 teaspoon salt

Preheat oven to 350 degrees. Butter a 2-quart shallow baking dish.

Steam the sweet potatoes in a steamer set over boiling water, covered, for 10 to 15 minutes, or just until tender. Cool them uncovered. Arrange the slices, slightly overlapping, in prepared baking dish.

Combine the brown sugar, butter, water and salt in a small sauce pan. Bring to a boil, then reduce heat to medium and simmer for 5 minutes. Drizzle the syrup over potatoes. Bake for 1-1/2 hours, or until the syrup is thickened and the potatoes are dark, golden brown.

This dish can be prepared a day ahead, covered and refrigerated. For serving, reheat in a 350 degree oven for 30 minutes. If desired, sprinkle miniature marshmallows on the top for the last 10 minutes. Serves 8.

Green Beans with Almonds

2 pounds fresh or frozen green beans
1/2 cup sliced, toasted almonds
1/2 cup butter

Cook the beans in boiling, salted water until tender. Drain thoroughly. Return to pot and add almonds and butter. Stir over low heat until butter is melted. Toss with the beans. Serves 8.

Is not old wine wholesomest, old pippins toothsomest,
old wood burn brightest, old linen wash whitest?
Old soldiers, sweethearts surest, and old lovers are soundest.

JOHN WEBSTER

Pumpkin Pie Squares

For the Crust:

1 cup flour
1/2 cup quick-cooking oatmeal
1/2 cup brown sugar
1/2 cup butter, at room temperature

Preheat oven to 350 degrees.

In a medium bowl, combine flour, oatmeal, 1/2 cup brown sugar and 1/2 cup butter. Blend until mixture is crumbly. Press into an ungreased 13-inch by 9-inch baking dish. Bake for 15 minutes.

For the Filling:

2 cups canned, plain pumpkin
1 13-ounce can evaporated milk
2 eggs
3/4 cup sugar
1 teaspoon cinnamon
1/2 teaspoon ground cloves
1/2 teaspoon ground ginger
1/2 teaspoon salt

In a medium bowl, combine pumpkin, milk, eggs, sugar, cinnamon, cloves, ginger and salt and stir until smooth. Remove the baked crust from the oven and pour filling on top. Return to the oven and bake an additional 20 minutes.

For the Topping:

1/2 cup brown sugar
1/2 cup chopped hazelnuts
2 tablespoons melted butter

Whipped cream

Combine the 1/2 cup brown sugar, hazelnuts and 2 tablespoons butter. Remove partially baked Pumpkin Pie Squares from the oven and sprinkle over filling. Return to oven and bake an additional 15 to 20 minutes or until filling is set. Remove from oven and cool at least 30 minutes in the pan. Cut into squares and serve with a dollop of whipped cream.

Microwave Mincemeat Filling

1 pound lean beef stew meat,
cut into 1-1/2-inch cubes
2 cups water
1 cup mixed candied fruit
1 cup raisins
1/2 cup currants
1-1/2 cups brown sugar
2/3 cup apple cider
2 teaspoons cinnamon
2 teaspoons ground nutmeg
1 teaspoon ground cloves
3/4 cup apple butter
3/4 cup cherry jam
3/4 cup orange marmalade
3/4 cup strawberry jam
1 cup canned sour cherries,
drained and chopped
1/3 cup Willamette Valley Vineyards
White Riesling
1/4 cup frozen orange juice
concentrate, undiluted
3 tablespoons melted butter
1/2 teaspoon salt

Pastry for two double-crust pies

Combine beef and water in a 2-quart microwave-safe casserole. Cover and microwave on high for 20 minutes. Stir and turn the meat, cover and microwave an additional 20 minutes, or until tender. Cool the meat slightly, reserving the liquid.

Grind the beef, candied fruit, raisins, and currants together through the large holes of a meat grinder. Do not use a food processor because it will liquefy the meat mixture.

Combine the brown sugar, apple cider, cinnamon, nutmeg and cloves in a 3-quart microwave-safe casserole and cook uncovered for 3 minutes. Stir until brown sugar dissolves.

Add the meat mixture and any reserved cooking liquid to the brown sugar mixture and stir well. Add apple butter, cherry jam, orange marmalade, strawberry jam, cherries, Willamette Valley Vineyards White Riesling, orange juice, butter and salt and stir until smooth. Cook, uncovered, in the microwave for 10 minutes. Stir and cook an additional 5 minutes, or until mixture comes to a full boil. Makes enough for two pies.

Roll out pastry dough on a lightly floured board. Fit dough in pie plate and prick all over with a fork. Fill with about 4 cups of mincemeat. Fit top crust on filling, seal edges together and crimp decoratively. Cut a few slits in the top crusts for steam vents and sprinkle a little sugar on top. Bake at 425 degrees for 10 minutes. Reduce oven to 350 and bake an additional 30 to 40 minutes or until golden brown.

I drank at every vine.
The last was like the first.
I came upon no wine
As wonderful as thirst.

MILLAY

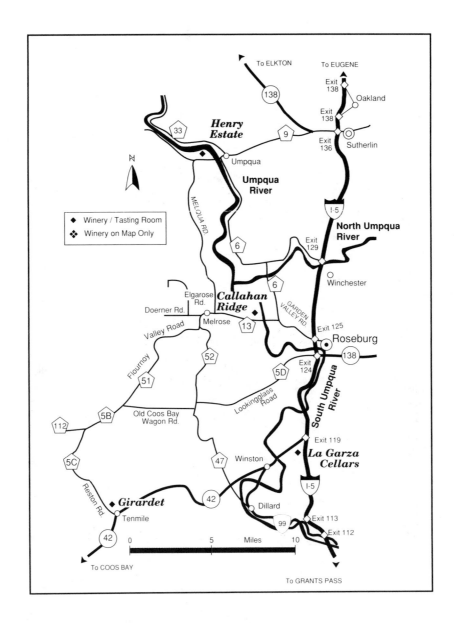

Umpqua Valley

Located just south of the Willamette Valley, and entirely within Douglas County in South-west Oregon, the Umpqua Valley covers an area approximately one-fourth the size of the Willamette Valley. The appellation extends west from the Cascades through and around Roseburg toward the Pacific Ocean. The valley is not a simple open basin, but an interconnected series of many small hillsides and river drainages known as the "hundred valleys of the Umpqua." The Umpqua Valley is drier and slightly warmer, as well as host to more varied soils, than the Willamette Valley. Temperature variations in this region are more exaggerated from daytime to nighttime, and from summer to winter. The characteristics of this appellation promote growth of a variety of winegrapes including Cabernet Sauvignon, Sauvignon Blanc, Chardonnay, Pinot Noir, and Riesling.

UMPQUA REGION

Menu

A Decadent Dionysian Midsummer Umpqua Feast

Callahan Ridge White Zinfandel
Smoked Salmon

———

Callahan Ridge Dry Gewürztraminer
Steamers

———

Callahan Ridge Chardonnay
Fish Baked in Parchment

———

Callahan Ridge Pinot Noir
Caraway and Garlic Stuffed Leg of Lamb
Fettucine with Gorgonzola and Walnuts

———

Callahan Ridge Dry Riesling
Mediterranean Vegetables

———

Callahan Ridge Cabernet Sauvignon
Aristotle's Coins

Callahan Ridge Winery

Founded in the Fall of 1987 by Frank Guido, Mary Sykes and winemaker Richard Mansfield, the Callahan Ridge winery has dedicated itself to the wines of the Umpqua Valley. In 1989, Frank passed away and in 1992 Joel and Kristine Goodwillie joined the winery as sales and promotions managers. Currently the four of them constitute the complete team at Callahan Ridge.

Located in a region where dry-farmed vineyards are the exclusive norm, Cabernet Sauvignon, White Riesling, Chardonnay and Pinot Noir thrive in soils ranging from decomposed red clay to shallow sandy topsoils above substrates of hard sandstone.

Viticulture has been practiced continuously in the Umpqua Valley since the late eighteenth century. Callahan Ridge is proud to be the purchaser of grapes from families claiming five generations of viticulture experience. It is a burden of honor to be entrusted with grapes from these families and Callahan Ridge has not taken this task lightly.

The wines are produced in styles classic to the old country. Winemaker Richard Mansfield, a graduate of Germany's school of enology in Geisenheim, has taken the time to acquaint himself with wines from all regions of the world. His experience in viticulture and enology serve him well when dealing with the grapes of the Umpqua Valley. Both the Germanic as well as the French styles of winemaking are pursued.

Callahan Ridge is one of the medium-sized wineries of Oregon. The 1993 production level was 18,500 cases. The wines are currently available in Oregon, Washington, British Columbia, Alberta, and Manitoba. Their plans for the future are to slowly expand to 40,000 cases while remaining a single appellation winery. Callahan Ridge is currently the largest purchaser of grapes in the Umpqua Valley. Projected new vineyard plantings should be able to supply Callahan Ridge with expansion requirements.

Callahan Ridge is currently farming a small demonstration plot (four and one half acres) adjacent to the winery. This vineyard has been farmed organically for the past four years and many of the local growers are using the experience gained at the home vineyard for their own operations.

CALLAHAN RIDGE
Oregon
Zinfandel
1992
UMPQUA VALLEY

PRODUCED & BOTTLED BY CALLAHAN RIDGE WINERY (BW-OR-124)
ROSEBURG, OREGON U.S.A   ALCOHOL CONTENT 15% BY VOLUME

Mankind possesses two supreme blessings. First is the goddess Demeter, or Earth—whichever name you choose to call her by. It was she who gave to man his nourishment of grain. But after her there came the son of Semele, who matched her present by inventing liquid wine as his gift to man. For filled with that good gift, suffering mankind forgets its grief; from it comes sleep; with it oblivion of the troubles of the day. There is no other medicine for misery.

EURIPIDES

Smoked Salmon

1 quart water
1/2 cup non-iodized salt
1/4 cup sugar
1/4 cup brown sugar
1 3-pound salmon filet,
    all bones removed
3 to 4 panfuls of hickory
    or alder chips

Combine water, salt, sugar and brown sugar in a large stainless steel, glass or other non-reactive bowl. Stir until salt and sugars dissolve. Add salmon to the brine and weigh down with a plate. Cover with plastic wrap and refrigerate 24 hours.

Remove salmon from brine and rinse lightly. Cut salmon to fit racks of smoker and allow to air dry for about 1 hour. Place racks in smoker and smoke the salmon according to manufacturer's directions for about 8 to 10 hours depending on thickness. Serve with cream cheese, capers and good bread.

Steamers

As a child, I would lie in bed on the south shore of Yaquina Bay listening to the mournful tone of the whistler guiding fishermen lucky enough to return home past the rough waters of the bar. The fog of the night and the aroma of the tidal estuaries evoked primal visions of steamer clams, Dungeness crab and succulent fish. The dry Gewürztraminer which I produce is my answer to these memories of clean seafoods and coastal mists.

Steam mussels, clams or crab in about 2 cups of Callahan Ridge Dry Gewürztraminer, 1 bay leaf and 1/4 teaspoon dry red pepper flakes. Reduce liquid by half and strain. Serve sauce with the seafood and good bread.

Fish Baked in Parchment

Butter and cheese require a wine with a rich acidity and the subtle vanilla flavors of French oak. Richard serves his Chardonnay with steaks of coarse-flaked fish (halibut, ling cod or cabazon), baked in a béchamel (let the sauce thicken during baking—saves time on the stove) with three thin slices of Walla Walla onion and a slight grating of nutmeg. Bake this enclosed in parchment until the fish is still moist and set but not dry.

Caraway and Garlic Stuffed Leg of Lamb

Have your butcher butterfly a 4 to 6 pound leg of lamb. Coat interior with 2 tablespoons caraway, a small handful of crushed garlic and a liberal amount of black pepper. Upend your bottle of general purpose olive oil over lamb and rub fiendishly. Roll and tie lamb with kitchen string. Repeat seasonings on the outside. Place fat-side up in a roasting pan. Roast at 325 degrees until internal temperature reaches 160 degrees, about 20 minutes per pound. Remove from oven and allow to stand for 15 minutes before carving. During that time, set the table, greet your guests and finish the bottle of Pinot which you probably have lying around the kitchen. I always have a few partial bottles on my countertop.

Fettucine with Gorgonzola and Walnuts

After two glasses of Callahan Ridge 1992 Pinot Noir, Richard, being suitably unencumbered, related the following recipe to me. He assured me that if one ate it Continental style (fork in left hand) there would be no calories. So follows his dream of the ideal food for his soft, non-tannin style of Pinot Noir.

Sauté 3 to 10 cloves of crushed garlic in 2 to 8 tablespoons of unsalted butter over low heat so the garlic does not burn. Remove garlic and discard. Melt 1/4 to 1/2 pound Gorgonzola (best) or simple bleu (in a pinch) in the garlic butter. Stir!

Thicken (or was it thin?) with Crème Fraiche (best), sour cream (good), or drained yogurt (gag, for the politically correct). Toss in 1/4 to 1/2 pound medium-finely chopped walnuts and serve over fresh fettucine.

And now, a short word from our winemaker. . .

Oh yeah, so I'm SORRY about all the many times I've cursed the judges at the various wine competitions. So now We've won a GOLD for our 1991 Cabernet. So all is roses and I'm running around kissing babies and shaking hands singing "happy days are here again" and maybe, just maybe the clouds will part just long enough to ripen this year's crop and I won't be standing in the rain dumping grapes in the press and coming down with the flu and not eating right and becoming frazzled when all the growers bring their grapes to the winery all at once and wondering why, just why didn't I heed my mother's advice and become a doctor or minister and then when the grapes have become wine I might, just might let out a sigh and look back on the harvest and think that it is times such as those that make it all worthwhile.

Ain't life grand?

Mediterranean Vegetables

In the heat of the summer one wants to spend as little time as possible over a hot stove. Richard Mansfield of the Callahan Ridge Winery related one of his solutions to quell the gnawings of the hungry tiger in the following recipe.

He sautées Mediterranean veggies in white wine (yellow and green zucchini, vine-ripened tomatoes, et cetera) in order of necessary cooking time, along with Mediterranean herbs—no garlic this time—merely thyme, oregano, rosemary, and lavender. Serve with crusty French bread and a high-acid, non-oaked white wine like his Callahan Ridge Dry Riesling.

Note: For a light one course summer meal, toss in a handful of scallops at the end of sauté, cover and remove immediately from the heat, keep covered and let stand for 5 minutes. Serve with vermicelli.

Aristotle's Coins

Richard developed this recipe one morning at about 1:00 a.m. prior to cooking for the 10th annual Umpqua Barrel Tasting Tour. His explanation of the name was that since Aristotle promulgated the theory of a geocentric universe where the cosmos revolved around the Earth, one taste of these coins would cause your mouth to become the center of all the cosmos and all other bodily sensations would merely orbit the taste buds.

For the Chocolate Coins:

12 ounces semi-sweet chocolate

Melt 12 ounces of the finest semi-sweet chocolate over hot, but not boiling water and then cool to 90 degrees while stirring constantly. Use a cake spatula to smooth over a baking sheet that has been covered with plastic wrap. Put in the refrigerator for 5 to 10 minutes to set the chocolate. Remove from the refrigerator and use a 1-inch round cookie cutter to punch out the coins. Return to refrigerator for 10 minutes then separate the coins from the surrounding chocolate by running hand under plastic wrap and pop them off. Store coins in freezer.

For the Mocha Cherry Ganache Topping:

12 ounces semi-sweet chocolate, chopped
1 pint heavy cream
4 tablespoons unsalted butter
3 tablespoons sugar
4 teaspoons cherry extract
2 teaspoons instant espresso powder dissolved in 1 tablespoon boiling water

Place chopped chocolate in a large bowl. Combine remaining ingredients in a medium sauce pan. Bring mixture to a boil and pour over chocolate. Whisk constantly until chocolate dissolves and mixture is smooth. Cool until mixture is firm enough to pipe. Fit pastry bag with a star tip and pipe Mocha Cherry Ganache Topping decoratively onto the Chocolate Coins. Chill before serving.

"Shall I call for a cab?" inquired Travis, the tall stranger to whom Jessica felt a mysterious attraction. "A cab. . ." she pondered; then turning toward him in her light evening gown she gently laid a hand upon his hand. . . "Only if it's Callahan Ridge Cabernet Sauvignon."

———

The late morning sun filtered in through the Venetian blinds and gently caressed Jessica awake.

She sat up. A smile crossed her face. "Had Nick really been so charming or had it been the Callahan Ridge White Zinfandel?" she thought. She arose, donned her cream silk peignoir, and went downstairs to squeeze orange juice for the two of them.

———

The tropical breeze sent warm fingers caressing the length of Jessica's sun bronzed body. A cloud passed over the sun as a tear trickled down her cheek.

"Tomorrow I must leave. Tomorrow; and I shall never see Renaldo again. Renaldo who had been so patient, so understanding, who had shared his Pinot with me, his Callahan Ridge Pinot.

"But I do know that I have some of that wine at home." The sun came out and, drying her tears, drove Jessica's sadness away.

———

"How *could* you!" cried Jessica as she hurled the Baccarat crystal vase at Brandon. "All your taste is in your mouth."

He ducked, barely in time to avoid acute cranial injury. "I didn't know it was so important!"

"Important!" she exclaimed. "You brought a *box* of wine, and it doesn't even have a cork! Don't you know Callahan Ridge White Riesling is the only wine I serve on my patio?"

———

Jessica, barefoot and clad in shorts and a light cotton blouse tied at the middle, opened the door to see a young man in an ill-fitting white shirt and tie. His bicycle leaned against her rose trellis.

"Excuse me, ma'am," he stammered, taken by Jessica's long golden red hair, green eyes, and tanned legs. "I'd like to talk to you about original sin."

Jessica gazed at the young man, causing him to blush. She thought of her cold bottle of Callahan Ridge White Zinfandel, Oregon's original Zin. "Yes, that would be nice," she said to him. "Please come inside."

———

Her heart pounding wildly, Jessica fell to her knees. Within the shadows hung the object of her desire. She reached out and brought it to her lips. A soft cry escaped her as the sweet nectar filled her mouth.

"Oh, Cal!" she moaned, so overcome with passion that she was unaware of anything other than the promise this grape held for the future of the Callahan Ridge Winery and the fine Chardonnay they would make from it.

———

"Here, let me help you with that," breathed Jessica. She leaned over and gently pried Mike's hands loose from the bottle of Callahan Ridge Cabernet Sauvignon.

Her long hair cascading over her face, she slipped the foil back, exposing the tan fine-grained cork.

Jessica looked up into Mike's half-closed eyes and with a rapid twisting motion, sank the corkscrew to it's hilt.

"No, please wait," pleaded Mike, "let me get wine glasses. I don't want you to spill any."

Jessica paused, but unable to hold back any longer, arched and pulled the cork from the bottle.

Callahan Ridge White Riesling

This wine has been styled in the manner of a classic German Spatlese. The wine exhibits a main aroma of peach-apricot with lower-level aromas which hint at the wines' crisp structure. The flavor is off dry, that is the wine is not dry. It is not cloying, however. The natural sweetness is balanced by a long and lingering acidity which renders the wine a perfect accompaniment to poultry, pork or game. In the same manner as a sweet sauce provides contrast to a dry meat—i.e. cranberry sauce with turkey, apple sauce with pork, or Cumberland sauce with venison, this wine is ideally suited to such foods. Naturally, the balanced sweetness allows this wine also to be enjoyed with only cheese, fruit and light breads.

Dry Riesling

Occasionally we decide to vinify one of four Rieslings in the dry Alsatian style. Selected yeasts are employed to ferment the last of the sugar out of the juice. These wines have a steely, almost flinty structure. Substantial fruit is still present to back up the crispness. Definitely Riesling, but unlike any Riesling you may have tasted elsewhere. These wines have the dryness of an Alsatian, the aromas of a good Rheinpfalz, and the steeliness of a Rheingau. We use them in conjunction with seafood marinara sauces, sautéed scallops, and chicken in Riesling (coq au Riesling). Many Chardonnay drinkers have walked out of the tasting room with numerous bottles of these wines!

Select Harvest White Riesling

In great years we allow one of our Riesling vineyards to hang long after the conclusion of the main harvest. The waiting can pay off when an infection of the noble fungus Botrytis sets in and an intense, straw-gold wine redolent of honey, peach and cedar may be born. These wines are of the quality and class of a great German Ausleses. The residual sweetness is scarcely noticeable, backed up as it is against the high acidity of these superb wines. Poached peaches on a raspberry sauce paired with such wines have been the highlight of many a winery meal.

Dry Gewürztraminer

The Gewürztraminer is a grape which is often produced into a sweet wine. Not so the Callahan Ridge Gewürztraminer! Bone dry yet with an interior richness our Gewürz has a fragrance of dusky rose petals, a soft acidity, and a long, never-ending finish. Oysters on the half-shell, boiled Dungeness crab, poached filet of fine-flaked dish, even a ceviche of bottom fish would be the ideal accompaniment to this wine. The Gewürztraminer benefits from aging and develops an incomparable depth after 6 to 8 years in the bottle.

Chardonnay

The Umpqua Valley is so similar to the French Macon, that our Chardonnay has often been mistaken for a French wine. Our Chardonnay hits full maturity every year, yet never requires irrigation. Delicate tropical fruit aromas, overlaid with the vanilla of new French oak delineate and define this wine. We use this wine whenever butter has been used in the preparation. Kris, the promotions manager, makes a killer linguini with clam sauce which causes our Chardonnay to sing arias.

Zinfandel

Some say that the closer one raises a grape to its natural northernmost limit, the more intense the flavor. Our first Red Zinfandel was produced in the banner 1992 year. Fifteen and a half percent alcohol, the wine surprisingly doesn't exhibit any indication of being too hot. The delightful caneberry aroma, intense yet balanced acidity, depth of flavor and tight yet yielding tannins give balance to this unbelievable wine. The wine is just a child, yet this child is already a prodigy.

White Zinfandel

Oregon's only example of this most popular wine, our White Zinfandel has a much longer finish than it's counterparts from the warmer regions to the south. A little softer than the White Riesling, it carries a slight natural effervescence. The White Zinfandel is the perfect summer patio wine. Since the wine is on the sweet side, it is recommended that it be coupled with foods which are on the salty side. Of all the wines produced by Callahan Ridge, it is the only one the crew drinks with ham or stir-fry. In fact, the last time beef-broccoli stir fry was served at Callahan Ridge, Richard had to return to the cellar twice to meet the demands of our table!

Cabernet Sauvignon

Some said it couldn't be done, raise a Cabernet in Oregon. We feel we have proven otherwise. The top award two years in a row at the Oregon State Fair commercial wine judging seems to cinched our claim to fame as one of Oregon's few producers of truly premium Cabernet Sauvignon. Deep cherries, warm vanilla and distinct yet soft tannins characterize our vintages. Definitely our choice for dishes of beef.

Pinot Noir

Oregon's flagship red, the grape which produces the great wines of Burgundy is just at home in the Umpqua Valley. Softer, not as tannic as it's brethren to the north, the Pinot from our winery is known more for the intensity of its fruit and the delicacy of its flavor. A short stay (five months) on French oak rounds and softens our Pinot without overwhelming it. Our wine of choice for leg of lamb with rosemary, garlic and black pepper (Douglas County is the lamb producing center of Oregon!). The wine is just as good when served with fettucine with Gorgonzola and walnuts, or chicken in Burgundy sauce—the traditional coq au vin.

Winter Warmer

Last, but by all means not least, is our most popular seasonal wine. Our winemaker took our good Pinot Noir, played around with a multitude of exotic herbs and spices and came up with a wine he used to enjoy when he was a student of winemaking in the old country. The Winter Warmer is designed to be served hot out of a mug in the cold of winter. It has its roots in the Alps where it is known as "Gluhwein." This wine is guaranteed to drive the chill out of winter cold toes, enliven a party and be the talk of all your friends. All that is necessary is to uncork the bottle, nuke it for four minutes and serve it with pleasure!

Menu

A French Bistro Supper

Girardet Riesling Estate
Crudité and Cheese Platter

———

Girardet Baco Noir
Pork and Hazelnut Terrine

———

Girardet Seyval Blanc
Gratin Dauphinois
Mixed Green Salad with Oil and Vinegar

———

Girardet Late Harvest Gewürztraminer
Tarte aux Pommes

Girardet Wine Cellars

Phillipe Girardet is a native of a small Swiss town at the headwaters of the Rhone, a French speaking region where winemaking is a centuries old tradition. It was there, in his uncle's vineyard, that Phillipe gained his first experience with winemaking, a love that would lead him to found the Girardet Wine Cellars in 1971. Yet it was not a straight road. At CalTech in the early 1960's, Phillipe worked as a design engineer. Then fate intervened. Phillipe met Bonnie, a beautiful young woman who had cultivated her own passion for the wines of Europe. They were married ten days later, romantic idealists to the very heart.

Such idealism and a lot of dreaming led them to Oregon in the late 1960's, where on a vacation up the coast they discovered the lush Umpqua Valley. The winery has since established a reputation for its collection of fruit, half of which are French cultivars. Girardet believes that French cultivars are especially good for the soul because they are very resistant to disease and as such require very few chemicals, creating a very pure wine. Their vineyard is virtually alone in producing Baco Noir, Marechal Foch and Seyval Blanc. Also produced are Chardonnay, Pinot Noir, Cabernet Sauvignon, Vin Rouge, Vin Blanc, Riesling, White Zinfandel, Gewürztraminer, and Country Rose. The grapes are harvested and fermented in small batches to ensure perfection and to maximize the opportunities to spot particularly choice fruits for a little creative experimenting. The personal, attentive approach is standard throughout the process. The duties of winemaking, such as sampling and evaluating, are shared by Phillipe and Bonnie Girardet and Patricia Green, an enologist. Their uncanny ability to create blended wines that are strikingly fruity with a delicate balance, such as is displayed in the Vin Blanc and Vin Rouge, has created pressure for the winery to expand production. Though one crush yielded 25,000 gallons and a number of others have approached this mark, Phillipe has chosen to continue producing small amounts of carefully crafted wines, keeping recent productions to about 15,000 gallons.

We have a busy lifestyle and five children, so we try to keep entertaining simple and informal. In the summer, we often eat supper outside at a picnic table under a grape arbor. The natural setting and the ease of preparation makes for a relaxed and pleasant mealtime, and it makes it easy to invite friends to stay at the last minute.

Crudité and Cheese Platter

Several French Cheeses
Feta or other goat cheese
Olives
Seasonal fresh vegetables,
    sliced into bite-sized pieces
Crackers

Arrange artistically on a platter and let your guests enjoy.

Pork and Hazelnut Terrine

This terrine is a make-ahead dish and can be kept in the refrigerator for a week.

1-1/2 pounds bulk pork sausage
    (lightly seasoned)
1-1/2 pounds braunschweiger
    OR other liver sausage
10 green onions, finely chopped
1 to 2 cloves garlic, minced
1/2 cup Girardet Chardonnay
3 tablespoons Cognac
3 tablespoons Port
2 teaspoons thyme
2 teaspoons marjoram
1 teaspoon oregano
1 teaspoon summer savory
1/2 teaspoon freshly ground
    black pepper
1/4 teaspoon allspice
1/4 teaspoon cinnamon
1/4 teaspoon cloves
1/4 teaspoon nutmeg
1/2 cup lightly toasted hazelnuts,
    chopped (reserve 1 tablespoon
    to sprinkle on top of terrine)

Preheat oven to 375 degrees.

Combine sausage and braunschweiger in a large bowl and break up with a heavy fork and knife. Blend together well with hands. Add remaining ingredients and blend again with hands. Press mixture firmly into a large (at least 10-cup) baking dish or terrine mold. Leave at least 1-inch of space at top. Sprinkle with reserved 1 tablespoon of chopped hazelnuts. Bake for about 1-1/2 hours, or until juices run clear when pierced with a skewer. Remove from oven and let cool for 1 hour. Cover with plastic wrap, place a weight on top (like a heavy can) and refrigerate for 1 to 2 days to allow the flavors to develop. Serve at room temperature with good French bread.

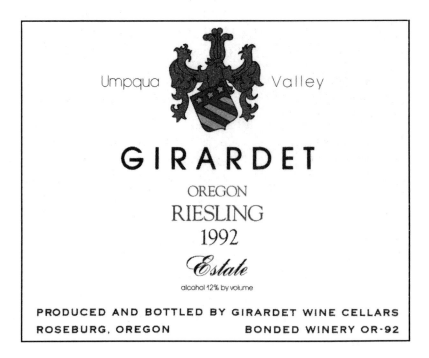

Umpqua   Valley

GIRARDET

OREGON
RIESLING
1992
Estate
alcohol 12% by volume

PRODUCED AND BOTTLED BY GIRARDET WINE CELLARS
ROSEBURG, OREGON   BONDED WINERY OR-92

> Like the best wine. . . that goeth down sweetly,
> causing the lips of those that are asleep to speak.
> THE BIBLE

Gratin Dauphinois

This recipe is from my husband's Swiss mother and is a very typical Swiss dish.

3 pounds russet potatoes, peeled and
    thinly sliced
2 cups grated Gruyère cheese
2 cups heavy cream OR milk for
    a less rich dish
Salt to taste

Preheat oven to 350 degrees. Lightly grease a baking dish large enough to hold all ingredients (this will bubble while baking).

Layer half the potatoes in prepared dish. Sprinkle with half the cheese. Pour in half of the cream. Sprinkle with salt. Repeat with remaining ingredients. Bake uncovered for about 50 to 60 minutes, or until potatoes are tender and crisp and golden on top. Serve immediately. Serves 6 to 8.

Tarte aux Pommes

This is a flat pie—actually a tarte—like you find all over France and the French side of Switzerland where my husband is from. It can be made with apples or any other fruit in season (good with fresh prunes, apricots and rhubarb).

Pastry for a one crust pie
4 to 5 apples, peeled, cored and
    sliced into thin wedges
3/4 cup heavy cream
2 egg yolks
4 tablespoons sugar

Preheat oven to 375 degrees.

Using your favorite pie crust recipe, roll dough out to fit a pizza pan, making a 1-inch high edge. Lay apple slices, slightly overlapping them, in concentric circles around the pie shell, all the way to the center. Blend the cream with the egg yolks and pour over apples. Sprinkle with sugar. Bake for about 40 minutes, or until the custard is set and the apples are nicely browned. Serve warm.

Menu

THE HENRY'S FAMILY
SUMMER SOIRÉE

Henry Estate Cabernet Sauvignon
Sylvia's
Teriyaki Steak

———

Henry Estate Pinot Noir
Scotty's Pinot Pesto Salmon
with Pasta

Garden Fresh
Corn on the Cob

———

*Henry Estate Select Cluster
White Riesling*
Grandma Henry's Fruit Pie
with a Lard Crust

Mimi's
Homemade Ice Cream

Henry Estate Winery

Scott Henry returned to the family homestead in the heart of the Umpqua Valley in 1972 after working as an aeronautical engineer in the California aerospace industry for thirteen years. He had observed, over a period of years, some of his friends enjoying their hobby of making wines. He and a long time friend, Gino Zepponi, scouted out the area in Southwestern Oregon as a possible grape growing region and then decided to try first hand raising wine grapes. The entire family helped plant the first twelve acres, consisting of Pinot Noir, Chardonnay, and Gewürztraminer, on land that has been owned and farmed by the Henry family for 75 years. An additional 23 acres have been planted since then, including three acres of White Riesling. For three years the grapes were sold to different wineries in the state. It was soon obvious that the decision to locate in the warmer, drier, Umpqua Valley (as compared to the Willamette) was a perfect choice. The more versatile climate combined with a multitude of soil geographies produces the most diversified growing region in the state. Realizing this potential, the Henry Estate Winery was built in 1978, just in time for crush. Scott hired Gino Zepponi as a winemaking consultant, and together they developed the distinctive wines of Henry Estate. The winery released its first wines in late 1980, and has had continuing success with its wine production ever since.

Continuing in the tradition of improving quality, Scott Henry has developed a unique trellising system that optimizes the maturity of grapes for production of world class wines. The "Scott Henry Vertical Trellis" is now widely used in many of the world's wine growing regions such as California, Long Island, New Zealand, Australia, and the Pacific Northwest. In 1987, the winery expanded its production from 6,000 to 12,000 cases per year in order to meet its ever-growing demand. An extension of the building was made that year and two new fermentation tanks were added to help handle the increased production. A major milestone came in 1988 when the Henry Estate Winery celebrated its tenth anniversary, launching it into a second decade of wine production as one of the state's oldest and most prestigious producers of Pinot Noir and Chardonnay.

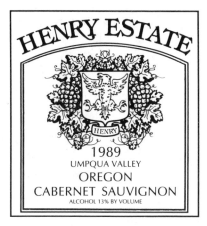

Sylvia's Teriyaki Steak

Sylvia Henry attended a summer session at the University of Hawaii, majoring in Oriental Cooking and "Underwater Basket Weaving." Her love of fun in the sun on the beach inspired this great recipe. This appetizer is requested on a regular basis by our family.

1 tablespoon sugar
1 tablespoon flour
1 teaspoon dry mustard
3/4 cup soy sauce
1/4 cup grated fresh ginger
1 clove garlic, minced
1 flank steak, sliced across the grain
    into 1/4-inch thick slices

In a medium sauce pan, combine sugar, flour and mustard. Whisk in soy sauce. Add ginger and garlic. Bring to a boil, then immediately remove from heat. Allow to cool completely.

Place sliced meat in a shallow dish and pour marinade over. Cover and refrigerate overnight. Thread meat onto skewers and grill over a barbecue. Serves 8.

Scotty's Pinot Pesto Salmon with Pasta

This recipe is a collaborative effort of Scott Henry IV, and his friend, Phil Gale. The combination of fresh salmon, sun-seasoned pesto, homemade pasta and a glass of Henry Estate Pinot Noir is a culinary delight.

For the Pinot Pesto:

3 cups fresh basil leaves
1/3 cup toasted pinenuts
    OR chopped walnuts
1/3 cup fresh Parmesan cheese, chopped
2 tablespoons lemon juice
3 cloves garlic, minced
1 teaspoon freshly ground pepper
1/2 teaspoon salt
1/2 cup olive oil

Combine basil, pinenuts, Parmesan, lemon juice, garlic, pepper and salt in the bowl of a food processor and process until smooth. Add olive oil in a thin stream until emulsified.

For the Pinot Pesto Salmon:

3 pounds salmon filets
1 cup Pesto
1/2 cup Henry Estate Pinot Noir

Whisk together the 1 cup Pesto and Henry Estate Pinot Noir until smooth. Place on top of the salmon filets. Let stand for 15 minutes. Grill over a medium grill for about 15 minutes, or until just cooked. The salmon should still be moist inside.

For the Pasta:

1 pound fettucine
1/2 cup Pinot Pesto

Cook the pasta according to package directions until al dente. Toss with 1/2 cup Pinot Pesto.

Divide pasta among 8 plates and place a portion of salmon on each plate. Serves 8.

Garden Fresh Corn on the Cob

There isn't anything better in this world than fresh corn on the cob. When Dad's garden starts putting out ears, we eat corn for lunch and dinner. Ahhh. . . sweet summertime.

Pick 8 ears of corn, husk them, boil them, roll them in butter, salt them and eat them.

Grandma Henry's Fruit Pie with a Lard Crust

To obtain this recipe, I had to do some persuading. Grandma has always made her pie dough by measuring in handfuls, dashes and sprinkles. By taking the time to measure out each ingredient, Grandma has given the opportunity to recreate her wonderful pie to many, who I am sure will enjoy it as our family has for years.

For the Fruit filling:

2 cups of fruit, cut into bite-sized
   pieces if necessary (any fruit
   can be used for this recipe)
1-1/2 cups sugar
1/4 cup flour
1 tablespoon butter

Preheat oven to 400 degrees.

In a large bowl, stir together the sugar and flour. Add the fruit and toss to coat.

For the Lard Crust:

1-1/2 cups flour
1 teaspoon salt
1/2 cup lard
5 tablespoons cold water

Mix flour and salt in a large bowl. Cut in lard until dough resembles the consistency of oatmeal. Stir in water until just combined. Divide dough in two and chill. Turn dough out onto a lightly floured board and roll out. Fit into an 8-inch pie plate. Fill with filling and dot with butter. Roll out top crust and fit onto pie. Crimp edges decoratively and cut steam vents in the top. Bake for about 45 minutes or until crust is golden brown.

Mimi's Homemade Ice Cream

6 egg whites
1/8 teaspoon salt
1/2 cup sugar
6 egg yolks
1 cup milk
1/2 cup light corn syrup
1 tablespoon vanilla extract
1 pint heavy cream
1/2 cup sugar

In a large bowl, beat egg whites and salt until stiff. Beat in 1/2 cup sugar.

In a separate bowl, beat egg yolks until light. Beat in milk, corn syrup and vanilla. Fold into egg white mixture.

In a separate bowl, beat heavy cream until stiff. Add 1/2 cup sugar gradually, and continue beating until sugar dissolves. Fold into egg white mixture. Pour into ice cream maker and freeze according to manufacturer's directions.

Menu

**Easter Dinner
(Dad's 75th Birthday)
For Eight**

La Garza Riesling
Crab Torte

**Crackers with Cream Cheese
and Smoked Salmon**

———

La Garza Chardonnay
**Green Salad Tossed
with Oregon Shrimp and
Vinaigrette**

———

La Garza Cabernet Sauvignon
**Garlic Stuffed Leg of
Lamb and Gravy**

Mashed Potatoes

Steamed Artichokes

———

*Your favorite
Oregon Sparkling Wine*
**Three Layer
Strawberry Shortcake**

La Garza Cellars

Donna Souza-Postles had worked off and on in the Oregon wine industry part time until 1986, when she took on a full time position managing another Umpqua Valley winery. Having gained the insight and experience to run a quality wine operation, she discussed with her brother, Cliff, the possibility of purchasing and restoring a facility in the Umpqua Valley that had become available. Knowing the financial needs of a winery, they decided to incorporate and include more family members, and in June of 1991 the Souza/Garcia family founded La Garza Cellars.

As Donna quickly learned, acquiring the winery was only the beginning of her challenges. Her pursuit of a restaurant to complement the winery faced red tape and numerous zoning hurdles. In February of 1992, the tasting room and wine shop opened at the winery; however, it took until September of 1992 before all the red tape could be handled and the Gourmet Kitchen added to the facility.

Today, the winery produces Cabernet Sauvignon, Merlot, Chardonnay and Riesling. In the spring of 1993, twelve acres of predominantly Chardonnay and Merlot were planted adding to the distinguished 3-1/2 acres of Cabernet Sauvignon that was planted in 1968.

Crab Torte

Pastry for single-crust pie
1/3 pound Jarlsberg OR Wisconsin
*   Swiss cheese, grated and divided*
1/3 pound Tillamook jalapeño jack
*   cheese, grated and divided*
1 pint ricotta cheese
3 eggs, lightly beaten
1/2 teaspoon marjoram
Meat from 1 large fully cooked
*   Dungeness crab, picked over*
*   for bits of shell*
4 green onions (including green part),
*   thinly sliced*

Preheat oven to 375 degrees.

Roll out your favorite unsweetened pie crust recipe and fit into a 10-inch tart pan with removable bottom. Prick all over with the tines of a fork. Sprinkle about 1/4 of the combined grated Jarlsberg and Tillamook cheese over the bottom. Chill until ready to use.

In a large bowl, blend together the ricotta, eggs and marjoram until smooth. Stir in 1/4 of the combined Jarlsberg and Tillamook cheese, crab and green onions. Spread mixture into prepared tart pan. Sprinkle with remaining grated Jarlsberg and Tillamook cheese.

Bake for about 30 minutes, or until filling is set and golden brown. Remove from oven and allow to cool. Remove from tart pan and slice in thin wedges. Serves 8.

The conscious water saw its God, and blushed.

RICHARD CRASHAW

Crackers with Cream Cheese and Smoked Salmon

1/3 pound cream cheese
1/4 to 1/3 cup sour cream
3 green onions (including the
*   green parts), minced*
32 of your favorite crackers
32 1-inch pieces smoked salmon

Place cream cheese and sour cream in a bowl and beat until smooth. Add just enough sour cream to thin mixture so you can pipe it through a large star tip. Stir in green onions. Lay crackers on a serving tray and pipe mixture decoratively onto crackers. Place a piece of smoked salmon on top of cream cheese "star." Serve immediately. Serves 8.

Green Salad Tossed with Oregon Shrimp and Vinaigrette

1 head curly leaf green lettuce,
washed, dried and torn into
bite-sized pieces
1 head red leaf lettuce, washed,
dried and torn into
bite-sized pieces
1/4 head red cabbage, thinly sliced
then chopped
1 large carrot, peeled and grated
8 hard cooked eggs, chilled, peeled
and sliced
1/3 pound cooked Oregon shrimp
meat
Tomato wedges OR cherry tomatoes
Italian vinaigrette dressing

In a large bowl, toss together lettuces, cabbage and carrot. Divide among 8 chilled salad plates. Place one sliced, hard cooked egg on each plate with slices overlapping. Divide shrimp among each plate. Garnish with tomato wedges. Just before serving, pour on your favorite Italian dressing. Serves 8.

Garlic Stuffed Leg of Lamb and Gravy

One 5 to 7 pound leg of lamb
6 to 8 cloves garlic, peeled and sliced
into thin slivers
Olive oil
Spike (a seasoned salt substitute)
2-1/2 cups water
3/4 cups flour

Preheat oven to 325 degrees.

Pierce lamb with a sharp paring knife, as you pull out the knife, insert a sliver of garlic. Repeat this procedure all over the leg of lamb. Lightly coat lamb with olive oil and sprinkle generously with Spike. Rub the lamb with the mixture. Place the lamb in a roasting pan and roast approximately 20 to 30 minutes per pound, or until a meat thermometer inserted into the thickest part of the meat reads 165 degrees for medium-rare. When lamb has 1/2 hour left to roast, pour 1 cup of the water into the roasting pan.

For the Gravy:

When lamb is done, remove to a heated platter and let sit 10 minutes before carving. Pour all drippings into a medium sauce pan over low heat. In a container with a lid, put in 1-1/2 cups cold water and 3/4 cup flour, cover, and shake well. Pour through a sieve into the simmering drippings, whisking constantly. Continue whisking until gravy is desired thickness. Pour into a gravy boat and serve over Mashed Potatoes (see page 146 for recipe).

Mashed Potatoes

10 large peeled and quartered
1/4 pound unsalted butter
Milk
Spike (a seasoned salt substitute)
Black pepper

Place potatoes in a large pot and cover with water. Bring to a boil, then reduce heat to medium, and simmer until potatoes are tender. Reserve 2/3 cup cooking water and drain off the rest. Mash potatoes and reserved water with a hand masher. Add butter to potatoes while mashing by hand. Now beat with an electric mixer adding milk until desired creaminess. Season with Spike and pepper to taste. Serve hot. Serves 8.

Steamed Artichokes

8 artichokes
16 cloves garlic, peeled and thinly
  sliced
Olive oil
Spike (a seasoned salt substitute)

Wash artichokes. Turn upside down and tap onto a hard surface to "open up" and loosen the leaves. Cut stems to 3/4-inch long. Cut top off with a serrated knife and discard tips. Cut tips off each leaf with kitchen shears and discard tips. Tuck 2 cloves of slivered garlic into the leaves of each artichoke. Lightly drizzle olive oil over each artichoke. Sprinkle generously with Spike. Place artichokes, stem side down, on the rack of steamer, and steam until a center leaf pulls easily from the artichoke and meat is very tender, approximately 30 to 45 minutes. Serves 8.

Three Layer Strawberry Shortcake

Make and assemble this cake first thing in the morning and chill in the refrigerator until served.

6 eggs, separated
1/2 teaspoon cream of tartar
1-1/4 cups sugar, divided
1/2 cup (1 cube) soy margarine,
    melted and cooled
1/2 cup water
Juice of 1/2 lemon
1 teaspoon vanilla extract
1/2 cup flour
1 tablespoon baking powder
1-1/2 pints heavy cream, whipped
    and sweetened to taste
27 strawberries, washed, hulled,
    sliced in half and sprinkled
    lightly with sugar

Preheat oven to 350 degrees. Lightly coat three round cake pans with non-stick spray.

Put egg whites and cream of tartar in a large bowl and beat until foamy. Continue to beat while adding 1/2 cup of the sugar, a few tablespoons at a time, until sugar dissolves and whites form stiff peaks. Place egg yolks in a medium bowl and slowly beat in melted margarine, water, lemon juice and vanilla extract. Continue beating and add remaining 3/4 cup sugar, flour and baking powder until smooth. Fold egg yolk mixture into egg whites. Divide batter between the three prepared pans. Bake for about 25 minutes, or until toothpick inserted in the center comes out clean. Remove from pans and cool completely.

To assemble, use 3/4 of whipped cream for the two bottom layers and the remaining 1/4 for the top. Use 9 strawberries (18 halves) per layer. Place one layer on a cake plate and spread whipped cream over. Press strawberry halves into whipped cream and cover with a little more whipped cream. Do not let whipped cream run down the sides. Place the next layer on top and gently press down. Repeat procedure. Place third layer on top and spread on remaining whipped cream evenly. Place strawberries decoratively on top. Scrape off any whipped cream that may have run down the sides. Chill until ready to serve. Serves 8.

Wel loved he garleek, onyons and eek lekes,
And for to drynken strong wyn, reed as blood.

CHAUCER

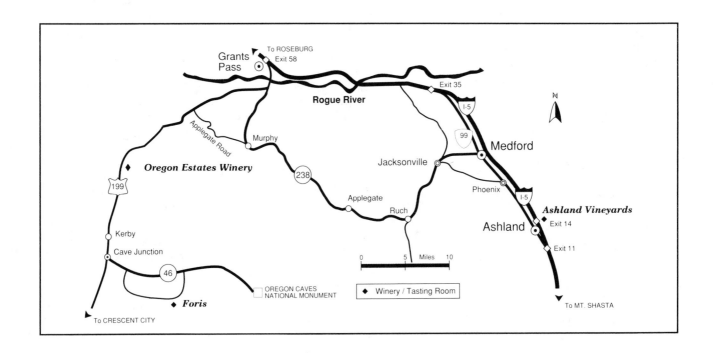

Rogue Valley

The Rogue Valley Appellation of Southern Oregon, situated at a higher elevation than the other winegrowing areas in the state, is composed of three distinct sub-appellations. The western-most Illinois Valley is strongly influenced by the marine climate of the Pacific Ocean and is host to the cooler climate varieties such as Pinot Noir and Pinot Gris. The Applegate Valley with a warmer climate is known for Cabernet Sauvignon and Merlot. Further inland and most sheltered from Pacific marine air is the Rogue River sub-appellation which extends from Ashland to Grants Pass along Interstate 5. Here, as well as in the Applegate Valley, the warm, dry climate is suitable for the production of most Bordeaux varieties. Chardonnay is grown throughout the appellation.

ROGUE REGION

Menu

McCully House Inn and Ashland Vineyards Winemaker's Dinner

Ashland Vineyards Sauvignon Blanc
Rock Shrimp "Coins" with
Ancho Chile Rémoulade

———

Ashland Vineyards Müller-Thurgau
Penn Cove Mussel and Asparagus Salad
with Chayote and Bok Choi Slaw and
a Nectarine "Mimosa" Vinaigrette

———

Ashland Vineyards Chardonnay
Rum Glazed Chicken and Smoked
Mozzarella Relleno on a Mango and
Vanilla Chardonnay Puree
with Pansies and Tortilla Rajas

———

Ashland Vineyards Merlot
Spinach Wrapped Lamb Tenderloin
with Morel Mushrooms, Riso
and a Merlot-Currant Reduction Sauce

———

Ashland Vineyards Cabernet Sauvignon
Grilled House-Made Sausages
on Port-Infused Black Beans
with Sweet Potato Torta
and Wood Roasted Peppers

———

*Ashland Vineyards Late Harvest
Sauvignon Blanc*

Ashland Vineyards
and Winery

The vineyards and winery property is comprised of 31 acres located just outside the town of Ashland in Southern Oregon. Sixteen acres are planted mostly in the Bordeaux varieties, which are particularly well-suited to the warm days and cool nights of Southern Oregon's Rogue Valley.

The winery grounds include a cottage-type tasting room, picnic area and ponds which are home to the winery's two swans, as well as a host of visiting wildlife and acres of unspoiled wildlife.

Ashland Vineyards' owner is former airline pilot Bill Knowles, who began construction in early 1988. The winery was completed in the summer of 1988 and first crush was fall of that year. The winery was constructed to specification and outfitted with the highest quality equipment available. Many of the vines were planted that first spring, with subsequent plantings each year. The Ashland Vineyards tasting room opened in the Spring of 1989.

The first releases were a 1988 White Pinot Noir, a dry blush wine made from 100% Pinot Noir grapes; and a Müller-Thurgau, an off-dry German-style white. These were followed by the 1988 Chardonnay and 1988 Pinot Noir in 1990.

In the summer of 1990, the winery introduced its first vintage of Cabernet Sauvignon. This 1988 Cabernet Sauvignon immediately gained notice because of its lush fruity style and supremely smooth drinkability. The winery's first Merlot, a 1990, was a gold medal winner at the American Wine competition in Chicago in 1993, and has received glowing reviews in several national publications. Subsequent vintages of these wines have proven the Rogue Valley's potential for growing great Bordeaux reds.

From the first six vintages produced at the winery, a total of 46 medals line the trophy wall of our tasting room.

The McCully House Inn is a 135-year-old Gothic Revival mansion and one of the six original buildings of Historic Jacksonville, site of Oregon's first gold discovery. The Inn is now the home of award winning Chef William Prahl and his "New World Cuisine." Chef Prahl has been featured in national magazines and was a participating chef at the prestigious "Masters of Food and Wine" held in Carmel, California.

Ashland Vineyards and The McCully House Inn joined forces and presented a five course Winemaker Dinner, which sold out for two consecutive nights. Winemaker Andy Swan and Chef Prahl first selected the wines to be served after the tasting, and Chef Prahl began the task of marrying his food to the wine. The recipes follow for your enjoyment.

Rock Shrimp "Coins" with Ancho Chile Rémoulade

6 tablespoons olive oil, in all
1/3 cup diced yellow onion
1/4 cup diced green bell pepper
1/2 teaspoon salt
1/4 teaspoon white pepper
3/4 cup chopped green onions
　　(including the green part)
1 tablespoon minced garlic
3 tablespoons Creole Seasoning
　　(see recipe on page 153), in total
3 large eggs
1 pound rock shrimp, peeled,
　　deveined and chopped
6 tablespoons freshly grated
　　Parmesan cheese
1-1/4 cups bread crumbs, in all
2 tablespoons coarse ground mustard
2/3 cup flour
1/4 cup water

Preheat oven to 350 degrees.

Heat 3 tablespoons of the olive oil in a sauté pan over medium-high heat. Add the onions, green pepper, salt and pepper for one minute. Add the green onions, garlic and 1 tablespoon plus 1 teaspoon of the Creole Seasoning (recipe on page 153) and cook for 1 minute. Remove to a medium stainless steel bowl.

Whisk 1 egg into cooked vegetables. Fold in shrimp meat, 1/4 cup bread crumbs, Parmesan and mustard and mix well. Set aside.

In a shallow bowl, combine flour and 1 tablespoon of the Creole Seasoning. In a separate shallow bowl, combine 1 cup bread crumbs and 2 teaspoons of the Creole Seasoning. In a separate shallow bowl whisk together 2 eggs and water.

Portion shrimp mixture into 1-ounce balls. Pack tightly, squeezing out any excess liquid. Roll each portion in the flour mixture; then the egg mixture; then the breadcrumb mixture. Flatten slightly and place on a tray.

Heat remaining 3 tablespoons olive oil in sauté pan over medium-high heat and brown shrimp cakes on one side. Turn over and place on baking sheet and bake for about 3 to 5 minutes or until cooked through.

Remove from oven and place 3 to 4 Shrimp Coins per person on a plate. Drizzle with Ancho Chile Rémoulade (recipe on page 153) and serve immediately. Serves 8.

Creole Seasoning:

2 tablespoons garlic powder
2 tablespoons paprika
2 tablespoons sea salt
1 tablespoon black pepper
1 tablespoon cayenne pepper
1 tablespoon ground coriander
1 tablespoon dried oregano
1 tablespoon onion powder
1 tablespoon dried thyme

Combine all ingredients and mix together well. Store in an air-tight container.

Ancho Chile Rémoulade:

1 Ancho chile
2 egg yolks
1 teaspoon dry mustard
1/4 teaspoon Kosher salt
1/2 to 2/3 cup olive oil
2 tablespoons lemon juice
1 tablespoon Champagne vinegar
2 tablespoons capers, rinsed
    and chopped
1/4 cup finely chopped celery
1/4 cup finely chopped yellow onion
1/4 cup finely chopped cornichons
1 tablespoon minced parsley
1 clove garlic, minced

Remove stem and seeds from the Ancho chile. Cover with water, completely submerged, and soak until soft. Place the softened chile in the bowl of a food processor and puree until smooth. Add egg yolks, mustard and salt and blend until smooth. With motor running, add oil in a thin stream, until emulsified. Blend in lemon juice and vinegar. Place in a bowl and stir in capers, celery, onion, cornichons, parsley and garlic. Mix well and chill before serving.

Penn Cove Mussel and Asparagus Salad with Chayote and Bok Choi Slaw and a Nectarine "Mimosa" Vinaigrette

For the Bok Choi Slaw:

2 chayote squash, shredded
1/2 head bok choi, thinly sliced
    diagonally
3 green onions, thinly sliced diagonally
1/4 cup rice wine vinegar
1 tablespoon sugar
1 teaspoon Sriracha Chili Sauce
    (available at Asian markets)

Combine chayote, bok choi and green onions in a medium bowl. Whisk together vinegar, sugar and Sriracha together and pour over slaw. Toss well and refrigerate several hours to allow flavors to marry, tossing occasionally.

For the Mussels:

3 tablespoons olive oil
1 celery rib, diced
1 small carrot, diced
1 small yellow onion, diced
1 cup Ashland Vineyards
    Müller-Thurgau
2 bay leaves
1 tablespoon peppercorns
20 mussels, cleaned and debearded

Heat olive oil in a pot large enough to hold the mussels over medium heat. Add celery, carrot and onion and sauté until golden. Deglaze pan with Ashland Vineyards Müller-Thurgau. Add bay leaves, peppercorns and mussels. Cover tightly and steam just until mussels open. Discard any unopened mussels. Remove mussels and cool. Reduce liquid by three fourths. Strain and reserve for Nectarine "Mimosa" Vinaigrette.

For the Nectarine "Mimosa" Vinaigrette:

1 cup Champagne
1/4 cup freshly squeezed orange juice
1-1/2 cups olive oil
1 nectarine, pitted and pureed in
    a blender or food processor
1/2 red bell pepper, seeded and
    finely diced
1 tablespoon minced shallot
1 teaspoon freshly ground pepper
Reserved mussel liquid

20 asparagus spears

Place Champagne and orange juice in a small sauce pan over medium heat and reduce to 1/2 cup. Remove from heat and whisk in olive oil. Place pureed nectarine, red bell pepper, shallots, pepper and reserved mussel liquid in a bowl. Pour in champagne mixture and whisk until blended. Refrigerate until needed.

Blanch asparagus in boiling water for 30 seconds. Refresh in ice water. Drain and towel dry. Divide asparagus between four plates in a fan shape with tips pointing out. Divide Bok Choi Slaw at the base of the stalks. Toss mussels with 1/2 of the Nectarine "Mimosa" Vinaigrette. Lean the mussels against the slaw, facing up. Drizzle remaining Nectarine "Mimosa" Vinaigrette across asparagus and serve. Serves 4.

Rum Glazed Chicken and Smoked Mozzarella Relleno on a Mango and Vanilla Chardonnay Puree with Pansies and Tortilla Rajas

For the Rum Glaze:

1/2 cup rum
1/2 cup soy sauce
1/4 cup sugar
Juice of 2 lemons
Zest of 4 lemons
2-1/2 tablespoons freshly ground
    black pepper
10 whole cloves, ground

Preheat oven to 350 degrees.

Whisk together all ingredients in a small sauce pan. Simmer over medium heat until mixture has reduced by two thirds. Mixture should be the consistency of honey. Set aside.

For the Rellenos:

1 pound boneless, skinless chicken
    breasts
3 tablespoons olive oil
2 teaspoons sea salt
1 tablespoon freshly ground pepper
1 tablespoon olive oil
1 cup diced celery
1/2 cup diced carrot
1/2 cup diced red bell pepper
1/2 cup diced red onion
2 jalapeño chilies, minced
2 chipotle chilies; seeded, soaked until
    rehydrated and minced
6 cloves garlic, minced
2 teaspoons cumin
1/2 cup sherry vinegar
1 cup chicken stock
1/4 cup Rum Glaze
1 cup grated smoked mozzarella cheese
1/2 cup bread crumbs
1/4 cup chopped cilantro
4 Poblano chilies, roasted

Place chicken breasts on a broiling pan. Drizzle with 3 tablespoons olive oil and season with salt and pepper. Broil until cooked through, about 5 minutes per side. Set aside to cool, then dice.

Heat 1 tablespoon olive oil in a skillet over medium heat. Add celery, carrot, red bell pepper, red onion, jalapeños, chipatoles, garlic, and cumin and sauté until just tender. Stir in sherry vinegar and simmer until liquid has reduced by half. Add chicken stock, 1/4 cup rum glaze and reserved chicken. Reduce slightly then stir in mozzarella and bread crumbs to bind. Fold in cilantro and adjust seasoning if necessary.

Carefully peel away skins from poblano chilies, keeping chilies intact. With a very sharp paring knife, slit chilies lengthwise along each chili and cut out seeds and seed cap. Keep stem intact.

Stuff chicken mixture into poblanos, taking care not to tear the chilies. Do not over stuff. Set aside until ready to bake.

For the Mango and Vanilla Chardonnay Sauce:

2 mangoes, peeled, seeded and chopped
1/2 cup Ashland Vineyards
    Chardonnay
2 tablespoons lime juice
1 teaspoon vanilla extract
2 flour tortillas, julienned and
    crisply fried
1/2 cup sour cream
12 pansy petals, minced

Puree mango in a food processor until smooth. Add Ashland Vineyards Chardonnay, lime juice and vanilla and blend well. Transfer sauce to a sauce pan and warm over low heat.

Bake Rellenos for 10 minutes or until heated through. Divide Mango and Vanilla Chardonnay Sauce between 4 plates. Top with 1 Relleno. Drizzle with sour cream. Divide Tortilla Rajas between each plate, placing them across stem end of chilies. Sprinkle with minced pansies and serve. Serves 4.

Spinach Wrapped Lamb Tenderloin with Morel Mushrooms, Riso and a Merlot-Currant Reduction Sauce

For the Merlot-Currant Sauce:

3 tablespoons olive oil
4 ounces bacon, diced
1 small yellow onion, diced
2 celery ribs, diced
1 carrot, peeled and diced
1 bay leaf
6 whole peppercorns
1/4 cup currants
3/4 cup red wine vinegar
1 tablespoon fresh rosemary
1 cup Ashland Vineyards Merlot
1-1/2 cups lamb stock
1/4 cup currants
2 tablespoons chilled unsalted butter

Heat the olive oil in a large sauce pan over medium-high heat. Add the bacon and sauté until cooked. Add the onion, celery, carrot, bay leaf, peppercorns and 1/4 cup currants and sauté until vegetables are golden. Stir in vinegar and rosemary and reduce until liquid is reduced by three fourths. Stir in the Ashland Vineyards Merlot and reduce to 3/4 cup. Stir in lamb stock and reduce to 1 cup. Strain sauce through a cheesecloth, pressing on the solids to extract as much liquid as possible. Discard the solids. Place sauce in a bowl set into a larger bowl of ice water to chill sauce. When cool, remove the fat layer on top. Place sauce in a small sauce pan and heat to a simmer over medium heat. Swirl in butter. Reduce heat to low and stir in remaining 1/4 cup currants. Keep warm until serving.

For the Riso:

3 cups lamb stock
1-1/2 cups riso OR orzo
    (rice-shaped pasta)
1 tablespoon fresh thyme leaves
2 cloves garlic
1/4 teaspoon sea salt

Bring lamb stock to a boil over high heat. Stir in riso, thyme and garlic and return to a boil. Reduce heat to medium-high and cook until pasta is al dente. Discard garlic. Season with salt and keep warm until serving.

For the Morel Mushrooms:

1 pound morel mushrooms,
    blanched and towel dried
2 tablespoons unsalted butter
1 tablespoon fresh thyme leaves
1/2 teaspoon freshly ground pepper
Sea salt to taste

Sauté the mushrooms in butter over medium heat until just tender. Season with thyme and pepper and salt. Keep warm until serving.

For the Spinach Wrapped Lamb:

4 lamb tenderloins
Salt and pepper to taste
8 ounces fresh spinach leaves; washed,
    dried and stems discarded
8 ounces caul fat, available from
    your butcher
1/4 cup olive oil

Preheat oven to 350 degrees.

Season lamb with salt and pepper. Divide the spinach leaves among the lamb and wrap each tenderloin. Divide the caul fat into four pieces and stretch them out on a work surface. Place spinach wrapped lamb at the end of caul fat and wrap the caul fat around the lamb, stretching the fat as you go. When lamb is completely wrapped, cut off excess fat and discard. Heat olive oil in a large skillet over medium heat. Brown the lamb on all sides. Place browned lamb in a roasting pan and finish cooking in the oven until medium-rare, about 5 to 10 minutes. Remove from oven and allow to rest for several minutes.

Divide the riso onto four plates. Place 1/4 of the sauce on the bottom half of each plate. Slice the lamb diagonally and place on the sauce. Top with mushrooms and serve. Serves 4.

I love everything that's old:
old friends, old times, old manners,
old books, old wine.

OLIVER GOLDSMITH

Grilled House-Made Sausages on Port-Infused Black Beans with Sweet Potato Torta and Wood Roasted Peppers

For the Sausage:

2 pounds boneless pork shoulder
3/4 pound fatback, available
    from your butcher
1/4 cup Ashland Vineyards
    Cabernet Sauvignon
2 jalapeño peppers, minced
1-1/2 tablespoons paprika
1 tablespoon Kosher salt
2 teaspoons minced garlic
1 teaspoon black pepper
2 teaspoons cayenne pepper
1 teaspoon chili powder
1 teaspoon coriander seeds,
    toasted and ground
1 teaspoon cumin seeds,
    toasted and ground
1 teaspoon oregano
1 teaspoon red pepper flakes
1 teaspoon sugar
3 feet of hog casings, washed well

Cube pork and fatback and put in a large bowl. Combine Ashland Vineyards Cabernet Sauvignon, jalapeños, paprika, salt, garlic, black pepper, cayenne, chili powder, coriander, cumin, oregano, red pepper flakes and sugar and add with pork and fatback. Mix well. Cover and refrigerate overnight.

Coarsely grind mixture twice through a meat grinder. Stuff into casings, do not overstuff. Refrigerate uncovered for an hour to dry slightly.

When the wine goes in, strange things come out.

SCHILLER

For the Port-Infused Black Beans:

3 cups black beans, soaked overnight
    then drained
2 tablespoons olive oil
4 ounces bacon, diced
1/2 red onion, diced
2 celery ribs, diced
1 small carrot, peeled and diced
1 red bell pepper, seeded and diced
1 poblano chile, seeded and diced
1 jalapeño pepper, seeded and minced
3 cloves garlic, minced
2 teaspoons cayenne
2 teaspoons cumin
1 gallon chicken stock
1/2 bottle Tawny Port
1 bay leaf
Salt and pepper to taste

In a large pot, heat olive oil over medium heat. Add bacon and sauté until cooked. Add onion, celery, carrot, bell pepper, poblano, jalapeño and garlic and sauté until soft. Add the drained beans and cook 1 minute. Add the cayenne and cumin and stir. Add the stock, port and bay leaf. Bring to a boil and skim off impurities from the surface. Reduce heat to low and simmer until tender. Remove from heat and allow beans to rest for 15 minutes.

Strain off excess liquid and pour liquid in a medium sauce pan. Simmer over medium heat until reduced by half. Return reduced liquid to beans. Adjust seasonings and keep warm until serving.

For the Sweet Potato Torta:

*1 sweet potato, peeled and
    thinly sliced*
*1 white potato, peeled and
    thinly sliced*
1/4 cup chopped fresh basil
3 cloves garlic, minced
1 tablespoon black pepper
1 tablespoon sea salt
1 tablespoon olive oil

Preheat oven to 350 degrees.

In a casserole dish, starting with the white potato, cover bottom of the dish in a single layer, overlapping slightly. Season with a little salt, pepper and basil. Top with a single layer of sweet potato. Season with a little salt, pepper and basil. Repeat process until all ingredients are used, ending with the white potato. Cover with foil and bake for 45 minutes, or until very tender. Remove from oven and place a weight on top of foil for 30 minutes to compress the potatoes so they hold together.

Carefully remove potatoes and cut into four portions. Heat olive oil in a large skillet over medium heat. Brown on one side. Turn over and place on a baking sheet. Return to the oven and bake an additional 10 minutes.

For the Wood Roasted Peppers:

2 red bell peppers
1 teaspoon olive oil
*Cherry wood or other wood
    of your choice*

Rub oil on peppers. Barbecue over cherry wood until lightly charred on all sides. Remove from grill and place in a tightly closed plastic bag for 15 minutes. Peel off charred skin and remove seeds. Discard skin and seeds. Slice peppers into 1/4-inch thick strips. Reserve.

Grill sausages until cooked through. Slice diagonally into 1/2-inch thick slices. Cover four plates with black beans, top with sliced sausages, a wedge of torta and top with pepper strips. Serves 4.

A feast of fat things,
a feast of wine on the lees.
THE BIBLE

Menu

A Grilled Feast at the Winery

Foris Vineyards Sparkling Brut
**Glazed Brie
with Fresh Flowers**

———

Foris Vineyards Gewürztraminer
**Spicy Spinach Salad
with Shrimp**

———

Foris Vineyards Vintage Pinot Noir
**Grilled Marinated
Salmon Filets**

**Grilled Fresh Garden
Vegetable Kabobs**

Calico Rice

**Warm Baguettes
with Garlic Butter Spread**

———

Foris Vineyards Pinot Gris
**Fresh Fruit
with Wine Gelée**

Foris Vineyards Winery

The fundamental philosophy at Foris is that winemaking begins in the vineyard, that less is better, and that experimentation in both field and winery are essential to attaining the highest quality wine. Ted and Meri Gerber, the winery's founders, have been growing Pinot Noir, Gewürztraminer, and Chardonnay for twenty years at Oregon's southernmost vineyard, deep in the Illinois Valley.

Foris Winery was built as a partnership between the Gerbers and Elizabeth and Russell Berard. The partnership has a combined vineyard planting of over 70 acres. Ted Gerber served as winemaker for an initial production of 5,000 cases per year. In 1991 Foris hired winemaker Sarah Powell. Sarah has experience in Burgundy, Bordeaux, South Africa, Australia, and Washington State. In the tradition of Foris, she is dedicated to quality and experimentation. Her recent awards, including the Governor's trophy—Best of Show at the 1993 Oregon State Fair with her 1991 Merlot—demonstrate the potential of the Rogue Valley as a grape growing region and have well displayed the talents of the Foris team.

Vineyard plantings of Pinot Gris and Pinot Blanc have expanded and Foris has also established the largest U.S. planting of the new and exciting Dijon clines. Production at Foris has grown to 11,000 cases of barrel fermented Chardonnay, Pinot Noir, Gewürztraminer, Cabernet Sauvignon, Merlot, Cabernet Franc and Méthode Champenoise, with plans to expand to over 20,000 cases within the next 5 years.

Glazed Brie with Fresh Flowers

1 cup vegetable stock
1 tablespoon dry white wine
1/2 envelope unflavored gelatin
1 8-inch wheel Brie cheese
Pesticide-free edible flowers and leaves
    such as: pansies, nasturtiums,
    violets, rose petals, rosemary
    and frambina leaves

In a small sauce pan combine stock and wine. Sprinkle gelatin over stock and wine and allow to soften for about 5 minutes. Place on medium heat and simmer until gelatin dissolves and mixture just comes to a boil. Refrigerate until cool but still liquid, about 1 hour. Remove from refrigerator and keep at room temperature.

Place Brie on a rack set in a baking sheet. Brush cool aspic over Brie. Decorate with flowers and leaves. Brush flowers and leaves gently with aspic to hold them in place. Refrigerate until decorations are set, about 45 minutes. Brush Brie with aspic and refrigerate twice more for a satiny sheen. Carefully arrange Brie on serving platter and serve with French Bread or crackers. Serves 6.

Spicy Spinach Salad with Shrimp

2/3 cup Foris Vineyards
    Gewürztraminer
1/4 cup soy sauce
1 tablespoon olive oil
2 teaspoons honey
1 teaspoon garlic powder
1/2 teaspoon grated fresh ginger
1/4 teaspoon red pepper flakes
25 to 30 cooked medium shrimp,
    shelled and deveined
2 bunches fresh spinach, washed well
2 tablespoons toasted sesame seeds

In a large bowl combine Foris Vineyards Gewürztraminer, soy sauce, olive oil, honey, garlic powder, ginger and red pepper flakes. Allow to stand for 30 minutes. Place shrimp in mixture and refrigerate an additional 30 minutes.

Wash and drain spinach well. Tear into bite-sized pieces. Place in a salad bowl and pour shrimp and dressing over spinach. Sprinkle with sesame seeds and toss well. Serves 6.

Grilled Marinated Salmon Filets

1/2 cup butter
1 cup brown sugar
1/4 cup lemon juice
1/4 cup Foris Vineyards Chardonnay
1-1/2 to 2 pounds salmon filets

Melt the butter in a small sauce pan over medium-low heat. Add the brown sugar and stir until dissolved. Add the lemon juice and wine and heat thoroughly.

Place filets in a shallow baking dish and pour marinade over. Refrigerate for 2 hours, turning occasionally. Grill over medium-low coals, skin-side down, basting with marinade until done. Serves 6.

Calico Rice

2 cups mixed rice, such as wild,
   long grain brown, sweet brown
   and red rice
4 cups vegetable stock
2 tablespoons butter
Salt to taste

Rinse rice. Place all ingredients in a medium sauce pan and bring to a boil. Reduce heat to low, cover tightly, and simmer for 45 minutes. Remove from heat and allow to sit covered for 10 minutes. Fluff with a fork and serve. Serves 6.

Grilled Fresh Garden Vegetable Kabobs

1 cup soy sauce
1/2 cup Foris Vineyards Chardonnay
1/4 cup honey
3 cloves garlic, minced
1 teaspoon grated fresh ginger
2 medium yellow crook-neck squash,
   cut into 1-inch pieces
2 medium zucchini, cut into
   1-inch pieces
2 red bell peppers, cut into
   1-inch pieces
2 medium onions, cut into
   1-inch pieces
1/2 pound medium mushrooms

Whisk together soy sauce, Foris Vineyards Chardonnay, honey, garlic and ginger in a large bowl. Place vegetables in marinade and refrigerate at least 1 hour, stirring occasionally. Thread vegetables alternately onto skewers. Grill over low coals, turning frequently, until vegetables are cooked and browned all over. Serve on a bed of Calico Rice. Serves 6.

Fill high the bowl with
Samian wine!

BYRON

Fresh Fruit with Wine Gelée

3/4 cup sugar
1-1/2 envelopes unflavored gelatin
2 cups Foris Vineyards Pinot Gris
2 cups coarsely chopped fresh fruit
   (honeydew melon, pears,
   strawberries, grapes, berries
   et cetera)
2 cups heavy cream, whipped

In a medium sauce pan, combine sugar and gelatin and mix well. Gradually stir in Foris Vineyards Pinot Gris, over medium heat, until gelatin dissolves and mixture just comes to a boil. Refrigerate for about 2 hours or until mixture is cooled but not set.

In a medium bowl combine fruit with aspic and mix gently. In six 6-ounce parfait glasses or wine glasses layer some of the fruit mixture then some of the whipped cream. Repeat layers. Refrigerate until set. Serves 6.

Menu

AN OREGON DINNER FOR FOUR

Oregon Estates Winery 1991
Chardonnay
Broiled
Marinated Shrimp

———

Oregon Estates Winery 1990
Pinot Noir
Barbecued Honeyed
Salmon Filets

Steamed Asparagus
with Cold Horseradish Sauce

Salad Vinaigrette

Rolls and Relishes

———

Oregon Estates Winery Iced
Dessert Wine
Strawberry Cheese Pie

Coffee and Mints

Oregon Estates Winery

Oregon Estates Winery is owned by the Seltzer family of Selma, Oregon, and the Dilley family of Eugene, Oregon. The vineyards are owned by the Seltzers and located in Selma; the business is managed from that location. The winery is located in Eugene and is primarily operated by the Dilleys. The vineyards were established in the winter of 1980 and consist of approximately 20 acres: 40% Pinot Noir, 20% Chardonnay, 20% Sauvignon Blanc, and 20% Cabernet Sauvignon. Small quantities of Riesling and Gewürztraminer were planted but are now available only as sweet dessert wines. In addition to still wines from the varietal grapes mentioned above, sparkling wine is also in Cuvée and will be on the market during 1994, as well as the first release of dessert wines.

Ralph and Irene Seltzer are Detroiters by birth, and both attended the University of Michigan. Ralph was educated as an attorney, practiced law in Detroit until 1963, then joined Motown Record Corporation in its very early days. He served there in various capacities, including director of the creative division, international director, assistant to the president, and ultimately for many years as vice-president of corporate affairs. In this capacity he was a friend and co-worker and dealt with such world-renowned recording artists as Stevie Wonder, Diana Ross, Marvin Gaye, the Four Tops, the Temptations, and was the person at Motown who was originally responsible for bringing the Jackson Five and Michael Jackson to that label.

The Seltzers raised four children in Detroit and ultimately moved to Los Angeles with Motown in 1972. After retiring from Motown in 1977, the Seltzers became enchanted with Southern Oregon and in 1980 moved to Selma, where they established their vineyard. Ralph has been active in the wine industry, having served as the first president of the Rogue Chapter of the Oregon Winegrowers Association, as two-term president of the Vice-Chair of the Oregon Wine Advisory Board, and currently serves on the Executive Committee of the United Oregon Horticulture Board (an advisory board to the Horticulture Department to Oregon State University) as the representative of the small fruit and grape industries.

Mike Dilley is the winemaker and has extensive background in the electronic media business, having commercially produced a variety of audio and visual presentations for such diverse clients as the South Willamette region of the Oregon Winegrowers Association, various micro-breweries, major lumber enterprises, and many other commercial enterprises. Mike also served for a number of years on the state board of the Oregon Winegrowers Association and was for several years the chair of the publications committee of that body.

Oregon Estates Winery was established in 1989 and its first release was that year. All wines are made 100% from the grapes grown at the Seltzers' vineyard in Selma, Oregon. The winery itself is located in a structure adjacent to winemaker Mike Dilley's residence in Eugene, Oregon. The grapes are crushed and destemmed at the vineyard and transported as liquid or must to the winery usually the same night as they are picked.

Broiled Marinated Shrimp

12 large shrimp, shelled and deveined
1 small bottle creamy French
    salad dressing
1 tablespoon minced garlic
12 toast rounds
1/2 cup grated Cheddar cheese

Fill a medium sauce pan halfway with water and bring to a boil. Blanch shrimp just until cooked, drain. In a medium bowl, whisk together French dressing and garlic. Add shrimp and stir to cover. Refrigerate at least 2 hours or overnight. Place shrimp on toast rounds and top each with a little cheese. Broil until cheese is melted and bubbly. Serve on small plates as a first course. Serves four.

Barbecued Honeyed Salmon Filets

1 side of salmon
Honey

Heat coals to high in barbecue. Grill salmon flesh side down first, then turn and brush liberally with honey. Continue grilling until done.

Steamed Asparagus with Cold Horseradish Sauce

3 tablespoons mayonnaise
3 tablespoons sour cream
1-1/2 teaspoons horseradish
1-1/2 teaspoons yellow mustard
1 pound asparagus, cleaned and
    trimmed

Whisk together mayonnaise, sour cream, horseradish and mustard. Chill until ready to serve. Steam asparagus until crisp-tender. Serve with chilled Horseradish Sauce.

Salad Vinaigrette

1/2 cup salad oil
2 tablespoons wine garlic vinegar
1-1/2 teaspoons minced fresh basil
1-1/2 teaspoons minced fresh parsley
1 teaspoon Dijon mustard
Salt and pepper to taste
Use a variety of salad greens,
    washed and dried
Olives, croutons, grated cheese,
    if desired

Whisk together oil, vinegar, basil, parsley, mustard and salt and pepper. Toss with salad greens and serve.

Strawberry Cheese Pie

For the Crust:

1 8-inch or 9-inch Danish rusk
1/2 cup butter, melted

Preheat oven to 400 degrees.

Place Danish rusk in the bowl of a food processor and grind to crumbs. Add butter until well combined. Press mixture into a pie plate. Bake at 400 degrees for about 3 minutes to set.

For the Filling:

2 8-ounce packages cream cheese
2 eggs
2/3 cup sugar
1 teaspoon vanilla extract
1/8 teaspoon salt

Preheat oven to 375 degrees.

Beat together cream cheese, eggs, sugar, vanilla and salt until smooth and pour into prebaked pie shell. Bake for 20 minutes, or until set. Remove and let rest on a rack for 10 to 15 minutes, or until cool to touch.

For the Topping:

Fresh whole strawberries, cleaned,
stemmed and well dried

Place whole strawberries, stem side down, in diminishing circles starting from the outside, until pie is completely covered.

For the Glaze:

1 cup strawberries, mashed
1 cup sugar
1 teaspoon lemon juice

Place mashed strawberries, 1 cup sugar and lemon juice in a medium sauce pan. Simmer over medium heat until slightly thick and clear, stirring often. Remove from heat and cool to warm. Pour glaze sparingly over top of strawberries. Chill Strawberry Cheese Pie for at least 6 hours or overnight.

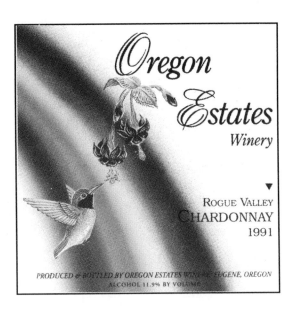

167

I rather like bad wine. . .
one gets so bored with good wine.

DISRAELI

Wineries in Oregon

ADAMS VINEYARD WINERY
1922 N.W. Pettygrove Street
Portland, OR 97209
Open Friday to Sunday,
noon to 6 p.m.
(503) 294-0606

AIRLIE WINERY
15305 Dunn Forest Road
Monmouth, OR 97361
Open weekends, noon to 5 p.m.
(503) 838-6013

ALPINE VINEYARDS
25904 Green Peak Road
Monroe, OR 97456
Open daily, noon to 5 p.m., after
September 15 open weekends
(503) 424-5851

AMITY VINEYARDS
18150 Amity Vineyards Road S.E.
Amity, OR 97101
Open daily, noon to 5 p.m.
(503) 835-2362

ARGYLE WINE CO.
691 Hwy. 99 W.
Dundee, OR 97115
Open daily, 11 a.m. to 5 p.m.
(503) 538-8520

ASHLAND VINEYARDS
2775 E. Main Street
Ashland, OR 97520
Open Tuesday to Sunday,
11 a.m. to 5 p.m.
(503) 488-0088

AUTUMN WIND VINEYARD
15225 North Valley Road
Newberg, OR 97132
Open weekends, noon to 5 p.m.
(503) 538-6931

BELLFOUNTAIN CELLARS
25041 Llewellyn Road
Corvallis, OR 97333
Call for hours
(503) 929-3162

BETHEL HEIGHTS VINEYARD
6060 Bethel Heights Road N.W.
Salem, OR 97304
Open weekends, 11 a.m. to 5 p.m.
(503) 581-2262

BRICK HOUSE VINEYARDS
18200 Lewis Rogers
Newberg, OR 97132
Open by appointment
(503) 538-5136

**BRIDGEVIEW VINEYARD
& WINERY**
4210 Holland Loop Road
Cave Junction, OR 97523
Open daily, 11 a.m. to 5 p.m.
(503) 592-4688

BROADLEY VINEYARDS
265 South 5th (Hwy. 99 W.)
Monroe, OR 97456
Open Monday to Friday,
11 a.m. to 4:30 p.m.
(503) 847-5934

CALLAHAN RIDGE WINERY
340 Busenbark Lane
Roseburg, OR 97470
Open daily, 11:30 a.m. to 5 p.m.
(503) 673-7901

CAMERON WINERY
8200 Worden Hill Road
Dundee, OR 97115
Open by appointment
(503) 538-0336

CHAMPOEG WINE CELLARS
10375 Champoeg Road N.E.
Aurora, OR 97002
Open daily, 11 a.m. to 6 p.m.
(503) 678-2144

CHATEAU BENOIT VINEYARDS
6580 N.E. Mineral Springs Road
Carlton, OR 97111
Open daily, 10 a.m. to 5 p.m.
(503) 864-2991

CHATEAU BIANCA
17495 Hwy. 22
Dallas, OR 97338
Open daily, noon to 6 p.m.
(503) 623-6181

CHATEAU LORANE
27415 Siuslaw River Road
Lorane, OR 97451
Open weekends, noon to 5 p.m.
or by appointment
(503) 942-8028

CHEHALEM
703 N. Main
Newberg, OR 97132
Open by appointment
(503) 538-4700

CLEAR CREEK DISTILLERY
1430 N.W. 23rd Street
Portland, OR 97210
Open by appointment
(503) 248-9470

COOPER MOUNTAIN VINEYARDS WINERY
9480 S.W. Grabhorn Road
Beaverton, OR 97007
Open Friday to Sunday,
noon to 5 p.m.
(503) 649-0027

CRISTOM VINEYARDS
6905 Spring Valley Road N.W.
Salem, OR 97304
Open daily, noon to 5 p.m.
(503) 375-3068

CUNEO CELLARS
9360 S.E. Eola Hills Road
Amity, OR 97101
Open Saturday, noon to 5 p.m.
and Sunday, 1 p.m. to 5 p.m. or
by appointment
(503) 835-2782

DUCK POND CELLARS
23145 Hwy. 99 W.
Dundee, OR 97115
Open Daily, 11 a.m. to 5 p.m.
(503) 538-3199

EDGEFIELD WINERY
2126 S.W. Halsey
Troutdale, OR 97060
Open Friday and Saturday, noon to
10 p.m. and Sunday to Thursday,
noon to 8 p.m.
(503) 665-2992

ELK COVE VINEYARDS
27751 N.W. Olson Road
Gaston, OR 97119
Open daily, 11 a.m. to 5 p.m.
(503) 985-7760

ELLENDALE WINERY
1 Main Street
Rickreall, OR 97371
Open Monday to Friday,
10 a.m. to 6 p.m. and weekends,
11 a.m. to 5 p.m.
(503) 623-6835

EOLA HILLS WINE CELLARS
501 S. Pacific Hwy
Rickreall, OR 97371
Open daily, noon to 5 p.m.
(503) 623-2405

EVESHAM WOOD WINERY
4035 Wallace Road N.W.
Salem, OR 97304
Open by appointment
(503) 371-8478

FLYNN VINEYARD
2200 W. Pacific Hwy.
Rickreall, OR 97371
Open Tuesday to Sunday,
11 a.m. to 5 p.m.
(503) 623-8683

FORIS VINEYARDS WINERY
654 Kendall Road
Cave Junction, OR 97523
Open daily, 11 a.m. to 5 p.m.
(503) 592-3752

GIRARDET WINE CELLARS
895 Reston Road
Roseburg, OR 97470
Open daily, noon to 5 p.m.
(503) 679-7252

GOLDEN VALLEY
98 E. 4th Street
McMinnville, OR 97218
Open Monday to Saturday,
11:30 a.m. to midnight,
Sunday, 2:00 p.m. to 10:00 p.m.
(503) 472-1921

HENRY ESTATE WINERY
687 Hubbard Creek Road
Umpqua, OR 97486
Open daily, 11 a.m. to 5 p.m.
(503) 459-5120

HILLCREST VINEYARD
240 Vineyard Lane
Roseburg, OR 97470
Open daily, 11 a.m. to 5 p.m.
(503) 673-3709

HINMAN VINEYARDS
27012 Briggs Hill Road
Eugene, OR 97405
Open daily, noon to 5 p.m.
(503) 345-1945

HONEYWOOD WINERY
1350 Hines Street S.E.
Salem, OR 97302
Open weekdays, 9 a.m. to 5 p.m.,
Saturday, 10 a.m. to 5 p.m.,
Sunday 1 p.m. to 5 p.m.
(503) 362-4111

HOOD RIVER VINEYARDS
4693 Westwood Drive
Hood River, OR 97031
Open daily, 11 a.m. to 5 p.m.
(503) 386-3772

JAMES SCOTT WINERY
27675 S.W. Ladd Hill Road
Sherwood, OR 97140
Open by appointment
(503) 452-7196

KNUDSEN ERATH WINERY
Worden Hill Road
Dundee, OR 97115
Open daily, 10:30 a.m. to 5:30 p.m.
(503) 538-3318

KRAMER VINEYARDS
26830 N.W. Olson Road
Gaston, OR 97119
Open Friday to Sunday,
noon to 5 p.m.
(503) 662-4545

KRISTIN HILL WINERY
3330 S.E. Amity-Dayton Hwy.
Amity, OR 97101
Open daily, noon to 5 p.m.
(503) 835-0850

LA GARZA CELLARS
491 Winery Lane
Roseburg, OR 97470
Open daily, 11 a.m. to 5 p.m.
(503) 679-9654

LANGE WINERY
18380 N.E. Buena Vista
Dundee, OR 97115
Open daily, 11 a.m. to 6 p.m.
(503) 538-6476

LAUREL RIDGE WINERY
46350 N.W. David Hill Road
Forest Grove, OR 97116
Open daily, noon to 5 p.m.
(503) 359-5436

LOOKINGGLASS WINERY
6561 Lookingglass Road
Roseburg, OR 97470
Call for hours
(503) 679-8198

MADRONA HILL VINEYARD AND WINERY
2412 N. Mississippi
Portland, OR 97227
Open Friday and Monday,
11:30 a.m. to 6 p.m.,
Saturday and Sunday,
noon to 6 p.m.
(503) 284-5153

MARQUAM HILL VINEYARDS WINERY
35803 S. Hwy. 213
Mollala, OR 97038
Open daily, 11 a.m. to 6 p.m.
(503) 829-6677

MCKINLAY VINEYARDS
7120 N.E. Earlwood Road
Newberg, OR 97132
Open by appointment
(503) 625-2534

MOMOKAWA SAKE LTD.
920 Elm Street
Forest Grove, OR 97116
Open daily, noon to 5 p.m.
(503) 357-7056

MONTINORE VINEYARDS
3663 S.W. Dilley Road
Forest Grove, OR 97116
Open daily, noon to 5 p.m.
(503) 359-5012

MOUNTAIN VIEW WINERY
22899 Alfalfa Market Road
Bend, OR 97701
Open by appointment
(503) 388-8339

NEHALEM BAY WINE CO.
34965 Hwy. 53
Nehalem, OR 97131
Open daily, 10 a.m. to 6 p.m.
(503) 368-9463

OAK GROVE ORCHARDS WINERY
6090 Crowley Road
Rickreall, OR 97371
Open Tuesday to Sunday,
noon to 6 p.m.
(503) 364-7052

OAK KNOLL WINERY
29700 S.W. Burkhalter Road
Hillsboro, OR 97123
Open Sunday to Friday,
noon to 5 p.m.,
Saturday, 11 a.m. to 5 p.m.
(503) 648-8198

ORCHARD HEIGHTS WINERY
6057 Orchard Heights Road N.W.
Salem, OR 97304
Open daily, noon to 5:30 p.m.
(503) 363-0375

OREGON ESTATES WINERY
1751 Draper Valley Road
Eugene, OR 97538
Not open to the public.
(503) 597-2161

PANTHER CREEK CELLARS
455 N. Irvine
McMinnville, OR 97128
Open by appointment
(503) 472-8080

PONZI VINEYARDS
14665 S.W. Winery Lane
Beaverton, OR 97007
Open weekends, noon to 5 p.m.,
weekdays, 10 a.m. to 5 p.m.
(503) 628-1227

RAINSONG VINEYARDS WINERY
92989 Templeton Road
Cheshire, OR 97419
Open most summer weekends,
noon to 5 p.m.
(503) 998-1786

REDHAWK VINEYARD
2995 Michigan City Avenue N.W.
Salem, OR 97302
Open Friday to Sunday, noon to 5 p.m.
(503) 362-1596

REX HILL VINEYARDS
30835 N. Hwy. 99W
Newberg, OR 97132
Open daily, 11 a.m. to 5 p.m.
(503) 538-0666

SAGA VINEYARDS
30815 S. Wall Street
Colton, OR 97017
Open by appointment
(503) 824-4600

SCHWARZENBERG VINEYARDS
11975 Smithfield Road
Dallas, OR 97338
Open Tuesday to Sunday, 11 a.m.
to 5 p.m., or by appointment
(503) 623-6420

SECRET HOUSE VINEYARDS WINERY
88324 Vineyard Lane
Veneta, OR 97487
Open Wednesday to Monday,
11 a.m. to 5 p.m.
(503) 935-3774

SERENDIPITY CELLARS WINERY
15275 Dunn Forest Road
Monmouth, OR 97361
Open Wednesday to Monday,
noon to 6 p.m.
(503) 838-4284

SEVEN HILLS WINERY
235 E. Broadway
Milton Freewater, OR 97862
Open by appointment
(503) 938-7710

SHAFER VINEYARD CELLARS
6200 N.W. Gales Creek Road
Forest Grove, OR 97116
Open weekends, 11 a.m. to 5 p.m.
(503) 357-6604

SHALLON WINERY
1598 Duane Street
Astoria, OR 97103
Open daily, noon to 6 p.m.
(503) 325-5978

SILVER FALLS WINERY
4972 Cascade Hwy S.E.
Sublimity, OR 97385
Call for hours
(503) 769-9463

SISKIYOU VINEYARDS
6220 Caves Hwy.
Cave Junction, OR 97523
Call for hours
(503) 592-3727

SOKOL BLOSSER WINERY
5000 Sokol Blosser Lane
Dundee, OR 97115
Open daily, 10:30 a.m. to 5:30 p.m.
(503) 864-2282

SPRINGHILL CELLARS
2920 N.W. Scenic Drive
Albany, OR 97321
Open weekends, 1 p.m. to 5 p.m.
(503) 928-1009

ST. INNOCENT WINERY
1360 Tandem Avenue
Salem, OR 97303
Open by appointment
(503) 378-1526

ST. JOSEF'S WINE CELLAR
28836 S. Barlow Road
Canby, OR 97013
Open Friday to Sunday,
noon to 5 p.m.,
or by appointment
(503) 651-3190

STANGELAND WINERY
8500 Hopewell Road
Salem, OR 97304
Open weekends, noon to 5 p.m.
(503) 581-0355

STARR AND BROWN
10610 N.W. St. Helens Road
Portland, OR 97231
Open weekends, 11 a.m. to 6 p.m.
(503) 289-5974

TEMPEST VINEYARDS
6000 Karla's Road
Amity, OR 97101
Open by appointment
(503) 835-2600

THE EYRIE VINEYARDS
935 E. 10th Street
McMinnville, OR 97218
Open by appointment
(503) 472-6315

THREE RIVERS WINERY
275 Country Club Road
Hood River, OR 97031
Open Monday to Saturday,
10 a.m. to 6 p.m.,
Sunday, noon to 6 p.m.
(503) 386-5453

TUALATIN VINEYARDS
10850 N.W. Seavey Road
Forest Grove, OR 97116
Open Monday to Friday,
10 a.m. to 4 p.m.,
weekends, noon to 5 p.m.
(503) 357-5005

TYEE WINE CELLARS
26335 Greenberry Road
Corvallis, OR 97333
Open Friday to Sunday,
noon to 5 p.m., or by appointment
(503) 753-8754

UMPQUA RIVER VINEYARDS
451 Hess Lane
Roseburg, OR 97470
Open weekends, noon to 5 p.m.
(503) 673-1975

VALLEY VIEW VINEYARD
1352 Applegate Road
Jacksonville, OR 97530
Open daily, 11 a.m. to 5 p.m.
(503) 899-8468

VERITAS VINEYARD WINERY
31190 N.E. Veritas Lane
Newberg, OR 97132
Open weekends, 11 a.m. to 5 p.m.
(503) 538-1470

WASSON BROTHERS WINERY
41901 Hwy. 26
Sandy, OR 97055
Open daily, 9 a.m. to 5 p.m.
(503) 668-3124

WEISINGER'S
3150 Siskiyou Boulevard
Ashland, OR 97520
Open daily, 11 a.m. to 6 p.m.
(503) 488-5989

WILLAMETTE VALLEY VINEYARDS
8800 Enchanted Way S.E.
Turner, OR 97392
Open daily, 11 a.m. to 6 p.m.
(503) 588-9463

WINE COUNTRY FARMS CELLARS
6855 Breyman Orchard Road
Dayton, OR 97114
Open daily, 11 a.m. to 5 p.m.
(503) 864-3446

WITNESS TREE VINEYARD
7111 Spring Valley Road N.W.
Salem, OR 97304
Open Tuesday to Sunday,
noon to 5 p.m.
(503) 585-7874

YAMHILL VALLEY VINEYARDS
16250 S.W. Oldsville Rd.
McMinnville, OR 97128
Open daily, 11 a.m. to 5 p.m.
(503) 843-3100

Index

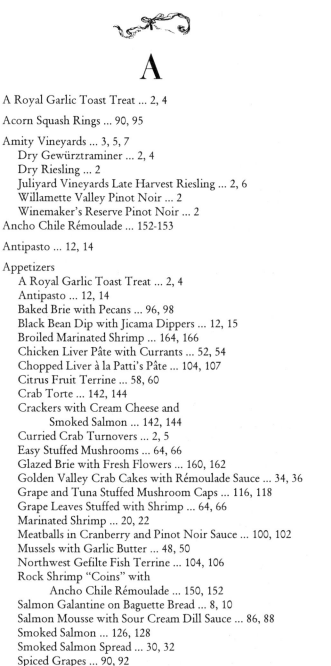

A

B

C

D

E

F

G

H

I

K

L

M

Q

R

Index

183

T

U

V